Collected Poems

For Kitty

Collected Poems
Leslie Norris

seren
is the book imprint of
Poetry Wales Press Ltd
Wyndham Street, Bridgend, Wales

© Leslie Norris, 1996
Reprinted 1999

The right of Leslie Norris to be identified as the Author
of this Work has been asserted in accordance with the
Copyright, Designs and Patents Act 1988.

ISBN 1-85411-132-9

A CIP record for this title is available from
the British Library

*The publisher works with the financial assistance of the
Arts Council of Wales*

Cover Painting: 'The Road to Aberystwyth' by John Elwyn

Printed in Plantin by
Creative Print and Design (Wales), Ebbw Vale

Contents

Water Voices

The Loud Winter

Autumn Elegy

September. The small summer hangs its suns
On the chestnuts, and the world bends slowly
Out of the year. On tiles of the low barns
The lingering swallows rest in this timely

Warmth, collecting it. Standing in the garden,
I too feel its generosity; but would not leave.
Time, time to lock the heart. Nothing is sudden
In Autumn, yet the long, ceremonial passion of

The year's death comes quickly enough
As firm veins shut on the sluggish blood
And the numberless protestations of the leaf
Are mapped on the air. Live wood

Was scarce and bony where I lived as a boy.
I am not accustomed to such opulent
Panoply of dying. Yet, if I stare
Unmoved at the flaunting, silent

Agony in the country before a resonant
Wind anneals it, I am not diminished, it is not
That I do not see well, do not exult,
But that I remember again what

Young men of my own time died
In the Spring of their living and could not turn
To this. They died in their flames, hard
War destroyed them. Now as the trees burn

In the beginning glory of Autumn
I sing for all green deaths as I remember
In their broken Mays, and turn
The years back for them, every red September.

The Old Age of Llywarch Hen

My crutch, see, Autumn is with us;
The fern burns red and harvest is in the house.
I have put away my strength and my promise.

I see in the evening the fire-smoke climb
And the earlier dusk send the children home
To their cool beds, their milk, their mothers' warm

Love in the hospitable house of youth
Where once I too had room and all the truth
I wanted was in four small walls. Now death

Examines everything I do. I need
A crutch, an abominable leg of wood
To hold me upright. I have a cold heart and a savage head.

Crutch there, do you hear the loud winter?
Young men go to the inn, singing as they enter,
But here in my room is the world's lonely centre

Where the voices of the young are the voices
Of ghosts. I know no young faces.
None come to see me. The young have their own places

In light and warmth and love. Which I knew
When my legs could carry me for two
Hill days and my breath was a long Halloo!

O my crutch, when spring was alive!
When loud were the undoing birds, like a dove
The smooth air. And girls offered their love

In all the bright Mays that a race of days
Chased past! Of all coloured plays
I remember these best. Old days, dead days.

Crutch, what if I burn you? Shall my age
Wither in the destroying flame, will my drudge
Body renew? It is a hopeless dream. I must trudge

Three-legged whatever ways are left, though rain
Renew the receptive fields. Stumbling and winter pain
Are what I know best. I'll not see Spring again.

Early Frost

We were warned about frost, yet all day the summer
Has wavered its heat above the empty stubble. Late
Bees hung their blunt weight,
Plump drops between those simplest wings, their leisure
An ignorance of frost.
My mind is full of the images of summer
And a liquid curlew calls from alps of air;

But the frost has come. Already under trees
Pockets of summer are dying, wide paths
Of the cold glow clean through the stricken thickets
And again I feel on my cheek the cut of winters
Dead. Once I awoke in a dark beyond moths
To a world still with freezing,
Hearing my father go to the yard for his ponies,

His hands full of frostnails to point their sliding
To a safe haul. I went to school,
Socks pulled over shoes for the streets' clear glass,
The early shops cautious, the tall
Classroom windows engraved by winter's chisel,
Fern, feather and flower that would not let the pale
Day through. We wrote in a cold fever for the morning

15

Play. Then boys in the exulting yard, ringing
Boots hard on winter, slapped with their polishing
Caps the arrows of their gliding, in steaming lines
Ran till they launched one by one
On the skills of ice their frail balance,
Sliding through time with not a fall in mind,
Their voices crying freely through such shouting

As the cold divided. I slid in the depth
Of the season till the swung bell sang us in.
Now insidious frost, its parched grains rubbing
At crannies, moved on our skin.
Our fingers died. Not the warmth
Of all my eight wide summers could keep me smiling.
The circle of the popping stove fell still

And we were early sped through the hurrying dark.
I ran through the bitterness on legs
That might have been brittle, my breath
Solid, grasping at stabs of bleak
Pain to gasp on. Winter branched in me, ice cracked
In my bleeding. When I fell through the teeth
Of the cold at my haven door I could not see

For locked tears, I could not feel the spent
Plenty of flames banked at the range,
Nor my father's hands as they roughed the blue
Of my knees. But I knew what he meant
With the love of his rueful laugh, and my true
World unfroze in a flood of happy crying,
As hot on my cheek as the sting of this present

Frost. I have stood too long in the orderly
Cold of the garden, I would not have again the death
Of that day come unasked as the comfortless dusk
Past the stakes of my fences. Yet these are my
Ghosts, they do not need to ask
For housing when the early frost comes down.
I take them in, all, to the settled warmth.

Snow

The snow surprised us, coming
  When it did,
A sudden white swarm, humming
  Out of the long cloud.
Winter, with a cold deciduous voice,
Came briskly and purposefully upon us,

And our secure horizon
  Retracted
To a warm room's bounds. But children
  Swanked into the yard,
Their warm laughter twirling the prodigal snow
Into peaks, columns, ghosts — the afternoon glow

Was evergreen memory for them.
  So we all,
Warmed, went to the window, away from
  The surly fire. The tall
Snow fell, and thicket, hedge and fence,
Familiar limits all, burned so with snow's radiance

As to delight, renew us.
  And we saw,
Thirty years clearer our eyes,
  Ourselves, puffed round with scarves,
Like rainbow robins bounce on the stiff-legged snow,
Innocently singing with voices lost long ago.

An Old House

Seeing him near the wall, I call my dog.
He lifts his head and its unholy eye.
An old dog knows the form and will not fall.
He moves towards me with a tolerant sigh,

An amiable dog. He shines against the light
His vigorous coat, and sits. Together we
Approach with care the fall I called him from,
Stop, and stare down. The river flushes by

Its melancholy brown. Old weeds, round stones
Are covered with its rusts down to the bend
Where, noisy as its cans, it disappears.
A bankrupt factory now holds the land

The old house owned, the house in which we played.
Rising in spasms from the ruined stairs,
The chastened sun was lost in puffs of dust
And the wild rooms moved coldly through their tears.

Caught in our play, we searched for that sad mark
The meek stabbed girl had at her murder made,
Running from sunlight into the vigilant dark.
That I was slow was not I was afraid,

But I did not believe. I heard my friends above
Run laughing through the green and peeling places,
In fungus rioting, in dry rot. The spent wood
Hung cobwebs from soft rafters in their faces.

And while I said I did, I could not see
How any struck girl in her ropes of blood
Could drive her thumb, soft palm, indelible whorl,
Inch deep into the stone before she died.

So when the voices stopped there came for me
A static moment out of time's command;
In that brief sky the impermanent birds still fly,
That mummied summer, still its airs suspend

In dead perfection, and ghosts put on their flesh.
For these are ghosts, the boys who from this house
Burst with hysteria in their spitting feet,
The whimpering ends of laughter in their mouths:

Then life caught up its breath, and I ran with them,
What they had seen I could not make them say.
In the harsh sun I found my freckled courage,
Jeered, was angry, went home a different way.

And walk a different way for a whole life.
Five simple years soon took them to the war
That burned their vision on all Europe's houses.
In the old house it was their death they saw.

After such roads I stand in the rind of the day
With my poor ghosts. Headlights stain the snow,
Light leaves the monotonous sky. Heavy with night,
Down the steep hill the wary motorists go,

Stiff on the packed ice. I whistle to my dog;
His eyes rejoice. The fall I call him from.
Now winter bellows through the travellers' air
And with a sigh I tell the dead go home.

The Ballad of Billy Rose

Outside Bristol Rovers Football Ground —
The date has gone from me, but not the day,
Nor how the dissenting flags in stiff array
Struck bravely out against the sky's grey round —

Near the Car Park then, past Austin and Ford,
Lagonda, Bentley, and a colourful patch
Of country coaches come in for the match
Was where I walked, having travelled the road

From Fishponds to watch Portsmouth in the Cup.
The Third Round, I believe. And I was filled
With the old excitement which had thrilled
Me so completely when, while growing up,

I went on Saturdays to match or fight.
Not only me; for thousands of us there
Strode forward eagerly, each man aware
Of tingling memory, anticipating delight.

We all marched forward, all except one man.
I saw him because he was paradoxically still,
A stone against the flood, face upright against us all,
Head bare, hoarse voice aloft, blind as a stone.

I knew him at once, despite his pathetic clothes;
Something in his stance, or his sturdy frame
Perhaps, I could even remember his name
Before I saw it on his blind-man's tray. Billy Rose.

And twenty forgetful years fell away at the sight.
Bare-kneed, dismayed, memory fled to the hub
Of Saturday violence, with friends to the Labour Club,
Watching the boxing on a sawdust summer night.

The boys' enclosure close to the shabby ring
Was where we stood, clenched in a resin world,
Spoke in cool voices, lounged, were artificially bored
During minor bouts. We paid threepence to go in.

Billy Rose fought there. He was top of the bill.
So brisk a fighter, so gallant, so precise!
Trim as a tree he stood for the ceremonies,
Then turned to meet George Morgan of Tirphil.

He had no chance. Courage was not enough,
Nor tight defence. Donald Davies was sick
And we threatened his cowardice with an embarrassed kick.
Ripped across both his eyes was Rose, but we were tough

And clapped him as they wrapped his blindness up
In busy towels, applauded the wave
He gave his executioners, cheered the brave
Blind man as he cleared with a jaunty hop

The top rope. I had forgotten that day
As if it were dead for ever, yet now I saw
The flowers of punched blood on the ring floor,
As bright as his name, I do not know

How long I stood with ghosts of the wild fists
And the cries of shaken boys long dead around me,
For struck to act at last, in terror and pity
I threw some frantic money, three treacherous pence —

And I cry at the memory — into his tray, and ran,
Entering the waves of the stadium like a drowning man.
Poor Billy Rose. God, he could fight
Before my three sharp coins knocked out his sight.

Picking Coal

I had thought until this late wind shook the wall
Winter had ended, but doors have banged all night
In the grumbling house,
Telling the sleepless about the entering weather.
A malignant cold, unwelcome, it turns the heart.

I remember a day like this, out of place in the warm
Young year. Frail sun licked the killed buds,
Ferns hung in the stopped
Threads of their fronds. Our breathing unseasonably
Flowered, we were walking the weather away.

Weather is all summer for boys in their confidence,
The sun inhabits them, their touch replenishes
What spoiled branches
They choose in their lucky vigour. But the land
So grown from our morning wishes, a blossoming country,

Was struck by abrupt black winter in a killing pyramid.
Our eyes could not fructify this. Death of the earth
Came in high cradles
From a harsh, close mine, on laborious wires,
Clumsily, inevitably. The dry axles' melancholy

Scraping squealed in the air like a disease of birds
And the heaped slag dropped, load on load,
Bones of the ripped pit's
Waste. Perched sliding, a man with his weak
Pick scratched among rattling for small knobs

Of lost coal, to warm in his sack. His long
Rags dragged in the dirt. He lived with winter.
Of his voice as he spoke
Across years and seasons through the cloud of his labour
I do not know, nor tell of his thin pale wrist

That no rubbed grime could strengthen. His decay grew
From the burned spoil where he stood. We were circled
By impregnable light and sun
And could not understand him, nor his sudden anger.
We offered him a cigarette from a rich packet,

But he refused, turning away with useless dignity.
It was golden David, so soon to die in exploding Europe,
Who lit up and smoked.
Now in my indolent, midsummer forties, hammocked in
        comfort,
It is this coldest wind disturbs, turning the heart.

Finding Gold

More Than Half Way There

Obsessed by night, my young voice told
Of swallows' ruby eyes between such trees
As the cool moon allowed, and their dark
Flight, elaborately simple, their desire
Unthinkingly perfect, and their perfect songs.

That was long ago. I use my nights for twitching
Sleep now, and what stern birds parade
In the iron trees do not disturb me.
I walk in the afternoons. The common
Blackbird sings and I accept this marvel.

To protect any true voice, even one like this,
Means constant vigilance. Each day I watch
An older hand take the food to my mouth.
I am alert lest an old voice soften
What needs to be said. Guard. Silence if necessary.

Dead Boys

Here is the field, beneath two hundred houses,
Where the boy
Buried a dead bird.
He felt for it a small, universal sadness,
And gave it a birthday sixpence, all he had.
Among these urban gardens his remembered tears
Are old now, and real as the unravelling breezes
That thirty years blew all his grief to dry.

The pond was here, its arid grains are laid
Higher than boys
About these flimsy garages.
All night long, all one long winter night,
The old tin Fords stood with their headlights turned
On its drowning ice, thin as a ripped sheet,
Where the covered slider lay in his silent bubbles
And would not be found. His school cap wrongly floated.

His name was known. The women sailed it
On gentle breath
Where they stood by the
Powerless cars in a darkness beyond rescue.
Gliding alone in the cold of a frozen death
He had not realised, the boy in his eyeless sight
Saw the face of the drowned, and held it
For simple mourning. He heard the desperate

Cursing of helpless fathers as weak ice kept
Them impotent.
Days are long to a boy;
Nights buried his foundered sadness in their tides
Till the black hulks slept in softness, as he slept.
Once he was thoughtless to an easy friend. The roads
Of summer led them away and they broke in a rough moment,
Never to meet again. It was here that he said goodbye

To his angular childhood. He walks the streets,
Their garish doors
Open to the field long gone,
And the grown man smiles as returning he meets,
In his eyed love, the cold, immortal children.
They run unblighted the green lanes of their time,
They laugh, their bright innocence unknown around them;
Here, where the field was, they live, the dead boys.

An Evening by the Lake

Well, let us admit it, I make
A pleasant picture here. A check
Overcoat, fresh from the cleaners,
Discreet suede shoes, (I use a wire brush),
Trouser-legs, that new bronze-green colour,
Just narrow enough for good taste.
I walk briskly, waving now and then and
Gently, a tweed hat.
Even my dog, unfashionable but
Successful, adds to my satisfaction.
She is obedient, but not servile.
On this grey evening, here at the edge
Of the lake and under the clouds,
She skips on the washed grass and is
Complacently white.
                          I have not lived
In the town for twenty years.

But walked this lakeside drive four times
A day when a boy, going to school
In a comic Gothic castle, built
For a fat iron-master. It turns
A stolid, limestone gaze down at
Me now.
                The park is quite deserted,
But for some poor boys, younger
Than I was, playing a thoughtless
Game a long way off. I watch them
Lift a great dressed stone, from
An old wall perhaps, stagger the few
Uneven yards to the water,
Then drop the huge thing in. I see
The little fountain of its drowning,
Then the slow circles spread. Boys' voices
Bounce to me over the resilient water.
Later I hear the stone's loud splash,

27

Much later.
     Four of us on this lake,
Using two boats, once rowed for the price
Of their hire a furious race. Off
To a gasped start, we plunged our oars
For all our thin arms' worth,
Driving the clumsy prows through
Burst reflections of the full clouds
And green banks. When I lifted my
Dripping blade from the water, (Dan
Chanting our time), I could see behind
The lovely dimpling of its leaving
The liquid skin.
     Then at last we stopped,
And called, our high voices skidding
Like flat, thrown stones over the resonant
Surface.
    Just like these later voices,
And this younger water, which have
Entered the locked cellar of my mind,
Broken its seal, and let its darkness
Out.
  So that I stand alone and
Bowed, on a scuffed, gravel path, in
A shabby park, my legs tired, my
Heart shaken, my jaunty clothes all
Wrong. All right, so my youth is dead.
And yes, those boys are gone.

A February Morning

This February morning, walking early to work
Across the frost-hung fields where the mild cattle
Stand wreathed in their own breath, I watch smooth
Starlings, loud handfuls of shot silk,
And hear my steps echo on the iron rime of the time.

Just as they echoed so sharply time out of mind ago
In my own country's cold
On the Dowlais moors at the dark of night
With one fierce unnatural star
Alone in the sky's arch.
Along the uncertain edge of the hanging mountain
The wild ponies limped and trembled,
Ice chiming like bells
In the long hair of their flanks. My footsteps,
Picked clean out of the cold and country air,
Hung their thin images on the ear's sharpness
For miles along the road
With never a near light nor comfortable sound.

But gently, and from no apparent direction,
The voice of a singing woman used the air,
Unhurried, passionate, clear, a voice of grief
Made quite impersonal by the night and hour.
For full five minutes' space along that mountain,
Not loudly nor ever fading away,
A full voice sang
Of such inhuman longing that I no more
Can say which was the song or which the fiery star.
One or the other lit the hollow road
That lay behind my clipped and winter steps
Time out of mind ago, in Wales.

This frosty morning, across the February fields
The militant bush of the sun in tawny splendour
Has not extinguished it, that song or star.

The Quarrel

Unable to sleep I turn from the comfortless bed
And watch where the night turns all our roofs to metal;
The world's inhuman now and has its consequent peace.
I see you sadly asleep on the grateful sheets
That are for me ropes, knouts, hard instruments;
I am glad of these circumstances. It is not long
Since my deliberate savagery made you desperate
And you waited too long for any contrition at all.

When I pretend that the best words come in the dark
And you are asleep as I speak them to the deaf moon,
For such dishonesty the night rejects my fever
And the malevolent furniture sneers from its corners.

Rain

Rain, bleak rain, is enough to set aside
The positive comfort of my solid roof;
Its harsh brush scrubs aside all
That I cannot see, the housed world
Is open to rain. I recognise
Its crepitations on my skin, its pocks
Slap hard on my neck. Gently, with
Unrelieved alarm, I feel my unwet
Flesh. I lie in the narrow
Warmth of the bed, hoping for the first
Tentative cry of the day-stirred
Blackbird, for the small thunder of the flying
Pigeons to carry the night away.

Elegy for Lyn James, killed in the ring at Shoreditch Town Hall, June 16th 1964

I saw your manager fight. He was
Useful, but his brother had the class.
In shabby halls in Wales, or in tents
On slum ground, I saw your like
Go cuffed and bleeding from a few
Sharp rounds to set the mob aloud
Before the big men came, who had the class.

Even they did not all escape. Tim
Sheehan, whose young heart burst
In a dirty room above a fish shop;
Jerry O'Neill, bobbing his old age
Through a confusion of scattered
Fists all down the High Street; brisk
Billy Rose, blind; all these I saw.

And Jock McAvoy, swinging his right
From a wheelchair. Your murderers hide
Fatly behind the black lines of the
Regulations, your futile hands are closed
In a gloveless death. Down rotting lanes,
Behind the silent billiard hall, I hear
Your shuffling ghost, who never had the class.

Alert

Rain mutters on the roof. I am alert
For God knows what unseemliness.
Last night my sleep was savaged
By creatures of my own failure,

Slunk out at last. I feel them cringe
Through the muffled care of my breathing.
I sit alert at the bolt-hole, not
Ready for fear, ears tense as a web.
Come in, come in, wherever you are.

The Strong Man

On my way to school I saw the man,
His little audience on the Square
Brought me abruptly running there.
Few on that boyhood afternoon
Had interest enough to spare,
Or money, to watch a rough tramp bare

To the waist perform his common tricks.
Incurious time had begun to wear
Haphazard patterns on his skin, to blur
The heavy flesh. He tore his packs
Of seedy cards, snapped through the air
The chains we'd thought as strong as care,

Leaving them empty on the ground.
Then, with a kind of wry despair,
He took a yard of iron bar,
Raised it, and brought it breaking down
On his own forearm. And over,
And over, boots kicking the floor,

The brisk tips sparking, until it had
Bent round his arm. His furious tonsure
Stung with sweat, his lips puffed lather,
The great ribs rasped. He stooped to the road
For his traps, his ripped shirt. We
Cheered his freedom: if such are free.

A Blunt Invasion

His name was Thompson, I am certain
Of that. Late from my homework, and with
Sufficient frost to set me off
Like Lovelock down the lanes
Of a fancied start,
I ran the roads
To find my friends.

Outside Ward's shop, where a happy light
Had warmed the dark stone for our play,
They stood in a sick silence. One
In distaste had turned away
To stare at the window.
Revealing nothing,
In a grim ring,

Not moving, the others thought of Thompson,
The impervious boy armed with a rough
Club of inch-thick paper rolled from the
Hoarding, who held them all in contemptuous
Balance, moving
Heavily, thick
Cudgel tapping,

Come up in his torn jersey from even poorer
Streets to state his value, his singular
Importance. After the conventional words
I slung my tight knuckles
Hard as a stone
Over his slow
Left shoulder

And the yellow blood ran stickily
Between his dirty fingers when he held
His agonised head. We looked without
Mercy at his tearless eyes.
He had a boil, he
Said stupidly,
A boil in his ear.

If I were to see him now, to see
Thompson now, I think we should smile,
A man's shared smile, knowing our lives
A blunt invasion of the better streets,
Our values
Challenged always,
Our triumphs accidents.

Rome Remembered

Wet on the slate roofs and the yard awash;
No football for the day. I looked from my desk
At two cold boys lost on the Welsh tips,
Their hands fumbling, their frail knees
Scarred as mine from too many a
Reckless fall, the drill rain
Needling incessantly their dark pelts,
Their round, dark heads.

From what deep mouth of their need
The she-wolf came I do not remember.
The ripped sack of her coat,
Her narrow legs, her cautious feet asprawl,
There she was
In all the loud smell of her dampness.
She covered her foul teeth, her brute head bowed.
The wolf is a poor creature at best.

But they recognised her animal rescue,
Her warm dugs grey as coal, and lived.
They turned from a whimpering den to build
On any seven of our hills a mythical city.
Rome stands in the raw towers
Of fallen steelworks, her eagle
Sails on the walls of sacked blast-furnaces,
Cinders cover her emperors.
Broken Remus is dead on the high moors.

A Sense of History

Walking at random over the mountainous moorland
With cry of curlew and wild mare's warning neigh
Held in an unhedged wind enough to knock your head off,
At the bitter end of a swept and solitary day

I came at last to the shores of an incongruous water
Perched without purpose upon a mountain summit.
The eastern end was a shelving bank of stone
And the terrible wind blew stiff waves upon it.

And, head down along the edge, I could not help notice
How all the long perimeter was similarly guarded
With single slices of stone, each patiently placed
Against the waves' water and into a crude mosaic.

Who dry-walled these shores? What men had planned
These back-breaking banks and lived on the low
Secure island? (It is there still, and still the stone
Ungainly circles that were houses how long ago).

I only know that I was suddenly kneeling —
While over me flew the torn, unheeding froth — .
And plugging with scales of stone the wave-worn gaps,
Ten frozen fingers against the loud storm's tooth.

Then heading homeward through the embracing marshland,
I faithfully found with quick and unearned skill
The hidden paths that led to the acquired valley,
Quite dry and hidden, away from wind, lake, hill.

Man and Boy

I and the white-faced boy I have to comfort
Walk in the lemon sunlight after our shadows,
He rocked with sobs and I talking kindly of nothing.

The afternoon train hurls its weight beyond the two meadows,
Leaving behind it a silence unbearably sad
Where the child is aloof and alone in his oval of grief,

His body bent, and his desolate landscape in tears.
For me the butterflies dance — and I hope he will see them —
Over the gardens where boys grow improbable flowers;

But winter's his world and something has broken his laughter.
So I keep him with me and we walk from the school to the
        gardens,
I walking alone, and he quite alone in his sorrow.

Soon he will stop and let the brave sunlight take over
The whole of his eyes, and flowers and butterflies prancing
Make up a new minute for generous summer to enter.

But I shall be left insidiously moved and troubled
As he runs through the playground kicking a stone before him,
Aware of my young despair and remembered terror.

He will cry in his sleep tonight, his small body turning
Through arcs of sadness that carry him out of his darkness:
I shall not cure his wounds, though my own scars are burning.

Gardening Gloves

Mild, knob-jointed, old,
They lie on the garage floor.
Scarred by the turn of a spade
In hard, agricultural wear
And soiled by seasonal mould
They *look* like animal skins —
Or imagine a gargoyle's hands.

But not my hands I'd swear,
Being large, rough and uncouth;
Yet the moment I pick them up
They assume an absurd truth,
They assert I have given them shape,
Making my hands the mirror
For their comfortable horror.

And I know if I put them on
I gain a deliberate skill,
An old, slow satisfaction
That is not mine at all
But sent down from other men.
Yes, dead men live again
In my reluctant skin.

I remember my father's hands,
How they moved as mine do now
While he took his jokes from the air
Like precise, comical birds.
These gloves are my proper wear.
We all preserve such lives.
I'm not sorry to have these gloves.

Looking at Snowdrops

Bursts through the rusty hedge the torn wind,
Turns, and with its last flap lifts
From their bent holds the ruffled finches,
Then softly drops them back
On other perches, bobbing, bobbing.

We walk past a cold bridge
In whose hard spars
A stiff girl clings that she may catch
Water's seductive shadows in
Her sharp viewfinder. A paperback
Hart Crane bumps in my jacket pocket
As I stump, chill, along.

When we see them, two fields away, great sheets
Of the small white snowdrops, my love,
Her eyes blazed by such urgent purity,
Exclaims them for water, sees them
Wide pools in the low grass, with small white waves
Genuinely gathered by the afternoon's cutting

Air. Now we step off the thin path
Among lakes of the flowers.
And this is disturbing. So might
That sauntering, sad Hart Crane, his
Solid boat set far homeward in the seapaths,
Have walked off into the waves,
Stepped no less easily into the deep sea, bobbing, bobbing,

Was drowned, yes, he was drowned.
In acres of white froth
And an orchard of rocks.

Siencyn ap Nicolas upon his Death-bed

Well, we all come to it. Siencyn, listen
to their cringing philosophies as the tears glisten
in the eyes of your punctual mourners.
I wish a plague would fasten

Their plump hides to my stale bed!
But anger will never lift my head
again from this foul pillow.
I have learned tolerance, that soft word,

however unwillingly. It is one of my late,
one of my few, virtues. I hate
the hypocrite who takes a pleasure
in his honesty. Many a desolate

truth I've undone with a kind
lie. And hope to be forgiven. We can't stand
all kinds of truth. If God calls for my
account I must ask Him to turn a blind

eye to truth's ledgers, for there
I have no credit. When I spare
time for plain speaking I make sure
I'm not believed. There is a wild humour

in the accidental, savage truth I use
that makes it fictional. Old men can choose
a kind of general truth that turns to wisdom
being void of malice. Not my way. But I'd not lose

a chance nobility I might, like a burr,
have picked on any casual road or moor
I've walked in my time. I'll not claim
merit for it. God's will. Found, not worked for.

Straight paths were never mine. When I was young
I let the hot blood take me where it stung.
God's doing, surely? He must know
His beautiful youths. I felt the sun

rise in my flushed veins, for the hot south
of life was in me and the songs my mouth
made then were many and easy. All roads
were mine for the laughing, and taking a breath

was like drinking wine. Yes, I remember
days when my five electric senses burned so clear
that I saw pale rainbows circumscribe the moon,
heard audible butterflies beat upon the air.

And the people I knew! A bright harmless
young man has friends everywhere. I witness
now that there was warmth on all the roads
for fifty miles and laughter in the villages

when I entered. And gave no thought to.
What's thought when the eager young are at their play?
Twin-faced I followed every tempting bend,
alone on the ecstatic hills, or roaring in company.

I eased my ways through the lanes, and the taverns
knew me well. Slept nights in the tall ferns
and laughed in the dark. Groped awake
in the smart mornings and ran to the barns.

Then, one evening, I felt myself taken,
my legs not my own, afraid and shaken
by an apprehension of power beyond
all I could guess, to a path on the mountain

where climbing through rowan and bracken —
I see it all still — I came to a broken
and absolute crest. In the world beneath
the bright farms went to sleep, and the moon

began in splendour her processional ceremony.
This was how I was called to my craft. I knew
from that moment that all must be seen and said,
that words not mine would seem to be

mine. I climbed the hill alone and left alone,
yet all around me tree and beast and stone
moved as I moved. The wary twigs stared.
Feathers of birds rooted at my shoulder-bone.

So I have walked the hills for what might have been lost.
I have seen the sun walk drenched out of the mist
of early morning, and dance on the hill-top. I have
been old as a stone the lichen has soundlessly kissed

and known all enduring life in inanimate things.
I have left my body and grasped the soft rungs
of the air. Trees and grasses live in me,
through me the long-dead sing again their songs.

Is this not Heaven? Yes, it is mine.
And therefore true. I was always one of Aristotle's men
for whom the ideal good is never pure
abstraction. We make our images warm, human,

looking on our own distortions kindly.
But I'll not reject any sly hope of a friendly
Heaven to come. Not that I've earned it.
No, I must enter by invitation only.

Now it is autumn and pigeons flock to the fields,
bald listless blackbirds lurk in the muddy laurels
and the heavy geese drive their high, frail wedges
into an iron sky. The birds are restless,

as I am restless, held in a filthy
cage of flesh, an old, sick man in a healthy
place, living his last on a rich son's
ready charity. Now in this wealthy

home I lie on a generous bed and feel
my life slide. I have sent away the girl
who came to read to me. To the young
nothing is simple. Why should my carrion smell

infect her innocence? Or my withered arm
misuse her compassion? Outside my room
the black weepers await my last
action. The ominous birds fly home.

And I must make my one way from
this shrivelled house of bones. I'll not welcome
Death, except in the way of courtesy.
I've loved in the world too long. But let him come.

Buzzard

With infinitely confident little variations of his finger-ends
He soothes the erratic winds.
He hangs on air's gap, then turns
On royal wing into his untouchable circle.
All, all, lie under his sifting eye,
The squat man, the sheep, the mouse in the slate cleft.

He is not without pity for he does not know pity.
He is a machine for killing; searchlight eye,
Immaculate wing, then talon and hook.
He kills without cruelty for he does not know cruelty.

If he fails in a small death he is awkward. And angry,
Loosing upon the hills his terrible, petulant cry.
To fail often is to die.
His livelihood is such single-minded and obsessional artistry.

He is not seduced by emotion
Or impeccable clear thought even
Into considerations other than his pure life.

We observe our prey doubtfully,
Behind many hedges and in tufted country.
Even when we see it clear
Have too many words to kill it.

Last Leaves

Late last night, the moon in puddles, I walked the lane
North from my gate up to the small wood where,
Stirring and trembling from the sentient trees,
The last leaves fell. I heard them in the still air
Snap. And almost saw their sifting passage down
To join their squelching fellows on the ground,
All glory gone. I tread on the black wreck
Of the year. Well, it is over.
Here, in full arboreal summer, struck
By the squinting light, I took for a hawk
No more than a flapping pigeon. I'll not make
That mistake in valid winter. No, I'll see
Each full-eyed owl stir not a breath
Of frost among the visible twigs as he pads
On air; and remember the owl's truth
For the vole, the silver frog, and the
Soft-bellied mouse, her summer breeding done.

Curlew

Dropped from the air at evening, this desolate call
Mocks us, who listen to its delicate non-humanity.
Dogs smile, cats flatter, cows regard us all
With eyes like those of ladies in a city,

So that we transfer to them familiar human virtues
To comfort and keep us safe. But this adamant bird
With the plaintive throat and curved, uneasy jaws
Crying creates a desert with a word

More terrible than chaos, and we stand at the edge
Of nothing. How shall we know its purpose, this wild bird,
Whose world is not confined by the linnets' hedge,
Whose mouth lets fly the appalling cry we heard?

Midwinter

A grey, flat sky and a flat land, squeezing
The eye of the north. Great blows of snow
Swing on a blind wind as the staggering
Morning lurches itself half alive. A beast
Could not stand alive now. What sparrows flew
Flocks deep long ago lie soft in their feathery dust,

Their frail twigs splintered as ice. Furrows
Are nailed to the ground by winter's iron
And lie, emptied of seeding. A desperate noise
Is lost somewhere in the width of the cold.
Houses lean to the violence and gasp, holding on.
A small house shoulders lower, grips firmly its hold

On whatever safety the rigid season offers,
So that its man, stung loud awake by treachery
Of the year, runs to make the small flames burn
In the dead wood of his hearth, turns his wet eye
Aghast at the rolling window. He hears
With pain his dry blood rustle, with a little groan.

Lunch at the Orlando

(for Ted Walker)

Lunch time as I leave
The building in which I work
Held up by generations
Of respectful polishing. Before me
The loud relief of students
Freed for the sunshine.
Their one wish seems to be
For a quick mediterranean tan.
Mine some beer and time slowing.

Walking through the park with the day
Alight, I see the first stub-tailed
Young swallows buttoned firm
On the perilous wires, or driving aloft
In flawless mastery of the alternative air.
Holy summer, so brief, now I fear the autumn.
The great white house gleams
That Georgian Hotham built to hold his title.
A clean hatter, Lady Jersey called him.

All playing children hold in their bouncing
Hands the sweet
Holiday bloom. It is as
A mortal ghost I make a way
Through the town, for nobody sees me.

Cheese rolls, ham rolls, generous
Mustard, two glasses of beer
Safely shaking on a table
Too small to shelter one's knees,
A sufficient order. We eye
With casual approval the pointed skill
Of the darts players, sneer tolerantly
At the worn drinkers too mild for words
Lapped in their gentle silences, their thoughts
Slow as fish.

      But however carefully I take
This uncold liquid, I feel its lake weight
Soon enough, and its physical alchemy.
By simple pressure only, it transforms me.
Hunched in gross uneasy leisure, my new Silenic
Physique uncouth around me, I am yet
Cautious I hope in my opinions.
Before my voice becomes too loud for confidence
I offer a tempered compliment here
Or a stiff judgement, imprisoning still
Those bitter sentences that all begin if only.

If only the unceasing birds
Were even momentarily still in the still skies if only
The translation of perception
Were made unforgettably perfect in concrete words
If only the sound of the true voice
Were not lost somewhere in the distorted throat
If only the naked moment were uniquely
Recognised.

      Well Ted, safe behind my eyes
The sentences lie locked these should have been.
What if the great lines never come; I have
The cold despair of searching for them.

We say goodbye and I heave my bay of beer
Past rows of hard brown pies on the slopping bar
Into the sunlight where shadows hard as tar
Sit in the corners, down to the sea.
The young have the sandy bloom
Of the season on them. Bands of lewd boys
Roam the sands, full of innocent knowledge.
If I were to shout here, it would be
Just another call, another call.
Gull-voice, bird voice, call of the lost sea.
My time complete, I turn away, turn back.

Concrete

You cannot carve it. With pat
Of grating shovel impress its
Thick embryo liquid, yes,
For garden paths where the cat's

Paws outlive their gentle tenant.
But find it everywhere; in tall
Tenements it frames the gloss
Of our living, supports the glass wall.

Once in a dressed street where
The midnight windows were black
And hid in a night of
Unlit neon the elegant neck

And turned wrist of each wax
Inhabitant of fashion, there flew
From the light of the natural moon
Four sparrows to their ledges. I saw

Their moulded buttresses as trees.
Fond birds, are you wrong to roost on concrete?
Men fashion its pillared strength, earthquakes
Can scatter it. Small grass can even pierce it.

The Old Year

Winter appoints its frosts, and the hedges blaze
With as many cold flames as light the tideless dark.
Ice holds the crackling ruts. I am reluctant
To leave the warm house, fooling that a soft book
Uses me seriously. Yet I should stand
Under a deep tree in a field of frost fire,
Hearing the call of owls, watching the rough old year
Gustily fronting its death with a brutal wind.

Day Trip from Hell

The years still rot then, the miserable
Erosion of the seasons. And unequivocal waves
Of the linked seas chart the graphs
Of time's shrinking. We marched to the Underworld
To a brass band beating time. All
This blueness! I have dreamed of a moment held
Longer than breath, infinity the blink of a short eye.

Aware of Death

At two-thirty in the morning I awoke choking,
Every fibre in my fur-lined lungs roaring
For relief of air, the room unhinged and bellowing

And the crazy window swimming in and out
Of two dabbed eyes. Take it easy, take it easy,
Said my unseated reason. Or feeble courage, I don't know.
Like hell, I thought, like hell I'll take it easy.
I began to nurse the oxygen like a miser,
Controlled the rasping walls with a shrewd squint,
Tucked rasping panic into an obscure corner,
And found I was easier. My arms for example.
I had thought them wildly pummelling the night for breath,
But they were confident on two clasped fists of sheet,
Calmly supporting my racked and labouring body.
I pulled carefully with my mouth at the painful
Air. It was like drinking straight out of a cold tap.

And nothing like this had ever happened to me before.

Later I lay for twenty minutes by the cold moon
In a metal sweat of fever, yes, but as well of
Almost the final terror, my lungs boiling,
Tongue too big for talk, mouth
Tasting the body's bitter dissolution;
Aware of death.

The Dove and the Tree

Night after empty night
I wait for the dove to descend
To its heart in the dark tree,
Fluttering wing and breast
(Wind-tremulous at flight's end)
Folded to slow love
Under the leaves of rest
And plain fruit's simplicity.

Diffident, urban, small,
The anchored garden lies
Chained to blind-flying night
And its passionate uncertainties.
Uneasy behind its wall
Of crumbling local stone
The lawn waits for the light.
The bird is above, alone.

Now sap in the bubbling wood,
Stung into sudden fire,
Illuminates each leaf
And vein of the tree's desire.
Spun to a tumbling flood,
Incendiary leaves leap high
And make of their own belief
A beacon for the sky.

The strumming summer trembles
Towards its ripe perfection
Among the purple grasses
And as each second passes
It gains a brief reflection
Thrown from the fiery tree
In phoenix agony;
And the heavy darkness crumbles.

Alone in the plumed air
Flies the plummeting blind dove.
Alive through its harsh despair,
The tree is alight with love.
The resinous tall flames
Their noisy pillars send
Into the ruffling clouds.
When will the bird descend?

When shall the bird descend
To her home in the landlocked tree?
I have no means to end

The intolerable tragedy,
But watch, aloof and sad,
Caught in its own distress
Beyond my wall their world
Dissolve in emptiness.

October Sun

Sun, wild October sun, unleash your lions.
Send them from brazen Africa, let them lean
Into my garden. (Even at night I know of
Those definite fences; there is deep slinking
Behind the water-butt).
Let them ignite the garage, let them enter
The house, leaving their yellow spoor
On the carpets. Let them invade my eyes,
I shall cage them behind my lashes.
Look, all the windows of my house are opened outwards
Look, my eyes are open.

Clymping, Sussex

I wait on the wet beach and watch the sun
Lie in a long blood on the reflecting sand.
I feel winter in a breath. Perpetual wind
Off the sea cold as gulls pulls down
To a lean crouch the marginal
Blackthorns and the bay turns round
Into a hard field. The brittle stubble ploughs
Its last year's lines. Then heavy woods inland,
In whose dark bush the copper pheasant crows.

Nightingales

1

My namesake, old Bill Norris, standing beneath a tree
So bitterly gnarled he might have grown from it, stopped
Talking to listen, lifted eyes dayblue and delighted,
And laughed a silent pleasure. 'There's a good many,'
He said, 'Walks past as close as you and never hears her,
Though she sings as bright in the hot noon as any night.'
Two feet above his head the dun bird pulsed and lilted.
It was in this village and perhaps for this same bird
I lay awake the whole of one miraculous darkness.
She sang so close to my house I could have touched
Her singing; I could not breathe through the aching silences.
And for nights after, hunched among pillows, I grabbed
At any sleep at all, hearing the nightingale
Hammer my plaintive rest with remorseless melody.
Full of resented ecstasy, I groaned nightlong in my bed.

2

Or driving one Sunday morning in Maytime Hampshire
On our way to a christening in one of the villages,
We stopped on Steep Hill, the road climbing headily upwards.
In the first warm air of the year we looked down on the
Trees, unmoving and full in the freshness of their leaves.
There were eight nightingales, eight, they filled the valley
With sobbing, the cataracts of their voices fell
Erratically among the splendid beeches. Open-eyed
We stood on the lip of the hill, while near and far
The water-notes of their singing grew faint, were lost almost,
Answered and redoubled near at hand, trailed
Dropping sadly down the valley-sides, struck purely out
With sound round notes into the listening morning.
We were still with music, as the day was. That we were late
For the christening was to the credit of those nightingales.

3

When I was very young my father took me from bed,
Dressed me in haste, and we walked into the night.
Winter was so long gone I had forgotten darkness.
We went by paths which in daylight knew me well,
But now were strange with shadow. It was not long
Before we came to the wood where the nightingale sang,
The unbelievable bird who lived in the stories
Of almost my every book. Would it sing, would it sing?
I thought the wood was full of silent listeners.
I do not remember it singing. My father carried me home,
My head rolling back on its stalk at every measure
Of his deep stride, and all I have brought back
From that long night are the fixed stars reeling.
It is the poet's bird, they say. Perhaps I took it home,
For here I am, raising my voice, scraping my throat raw again.

Driving Home

The first bite of the engine scares
An old blackbird. He flares
Off into his laurels, comic fear
Ruffles his feathers. In first gear
I gentle the car, fingertip
Its huge waiting idly up,
Then a touch,
Snick, into second past the curbed clutch,
Flick a glance at a bus,
Slide, so obviously without fuss
It becomes a tactfully pretentious
Act, cosily into the relevant
Traffic. In front
Is an old Alvis; nice. My hands wear
Their driving leather.

Today is the last of the working year
And winter rain expected weather.
With some panache I engage the windscreen wiper.

In third onto the dual carriage-way.
Foot down, the cool snarl unfurls my
Gritty nerves, then velvet into top
And the free straight.
We swing at the bend
On a smooth string's end
And gobble for home, battering the rain
To the bucketing gutters
In enormous waves, like music. At once a strain,
A swell, and incredulous orchestras
Play sticky crescendos from remembered cinemas
All through the village. A rope
Of water, twined by speed,
Winds like a tune down the side
Window as I sober the brake,
Change down; I make
The curved drive
With a noise like surf.
I am home in the pale wet.

And in my room I wait,
Having turned from the window and the late
Light. Here I can see
The total uncertainty that belongs to me,
Old letters, old papers, a book
Thrown to the floor,
A confusion of effort that means no more
To me now than the common music
I brought home in the car,
The soiled detritus of a whole year's war
Against myself, against my dying leaves.
No man can do this for me, I can pay
No man, and wearily I begin
To jostle into order overrun
Good intentions thrown away

Long ago. Shrugging with amused distaste
At the shabby evidence, the waste
Of eagerness, the death of time,
I put my books back on their sightless shelves.
When I have done I will sit in the orderly dark,
Waiting for what will come to me, what is to come.

Finding Gold

From his house each day the child moves to school
Through a deliberate ceremony. He is obsessed
By a chosen maze, marking his ritual
With clear jumps over long stones full
Of inescapable bad luck, then a stick's rattle
Briskly along twenty-three exact bars of tall
Fence outside the bus station; the road crossed
Here, always. His frail, unswerving rule
Is to impose order on a chaotic world.

Pressed by his abiding route, he mounts the stone
Parapet. One step to the edge and, elate
With danger, coldly he stares down at
The diminished water. Freckled mallows fret
At the shallow runs. Slowly, slowly now, must
He turn and saunter with rehearsed arrogance the lane
Through the sagging garages, slack doors on the yawn.
He will not move his head when shadows threaten,
Nor falter a slid inch from his restricted cobbles.

But here in a sunny gap between two sheds
Is a circle of stone seats, loosely deserted.
Black as police stand the rough walls, the gamblers
Are running down tittering alleys, their cards
Scattered as windfalls, their copper bets
Spilled in fallen coils. The quick child

Hurries deep coins into the crannies of his pockets
And breaks for school. All safe custom run wild,
He laughs in the tumble of the anonymous playground.

All day he sat in school, full of pennies
To his round eyes. He thought without moving
Of springing circles of stone standing inches
Outside his orderly magic, and knew for us
All, one step from broken practice the spread gold lies,
In the green lanes of absence. Are his coins living?
Does he stride on the mapless hills where the gamblers'
Dust is lifted? Is he stumping his trodden roads
With an old day turning, stupidly turning?

Ransoms

Cardigan Bay

(for Kitty)

The buzzard hung crossed
On the air and we came
Down from the hills under
Him. First sun from
The underworld turned
White his stretched surfaces,
Whitened the cracked stone

On this beach where end
The works of the sea,
The total husbandry
Of water. Now at noon
We walk the land between
The seamarks, knowing

That wave already made
To wash away our happy
Loitering before
We turn back into evening
Among the frail daffodils
Growing in other seasons.

For those who live here
After our daylight, I
Could wish us to look
Out of the darkness
We have become, teaching
Them happiness, a true love.

Water

On hot summer mornings my aunt set glasses
On a low wall outside the farmhouse,
With some jugs of cold water.
I would sit in the dark hall, or
        Behind the dairy window,
Waiting for children to come from the town.

They came in small groups, serious, steady,
And I could see them, black in the heat,
Long before they turned in at our gate
To march up the soft, dirt road.
        They would stand by the wall,
Drinking water with an engrossed thirst. The dog

Did not bother them, knowing them responsible
Travellers. They held in quiet hands their bags
Of jam sandwiches, and bottles of yellow fizz.
Sometimes they waved a gratitude to the house,
        But they never looked at us.
Their eyes were full of the mountain, lifting

Their measuring faces above our long hedge.
When they had gone I would climb the wall,
Looking for them among the thin sheep runs.
Their heads were a resolute darkness among ferns,
        They climbed with unsteady certainty.
I wondered what it was they knew the mountain had.

They would pass the last house, Lambert's, where
A violent gander, too old by many a Christmas,
Blared evil warning from his bitten moor,
Then it was open world, too high and clear
        For clouds even, where over heather
The free hare cleanly ran, and the summer sheep.

I knew this; and I knew all summer long
Those visionary gangs passed through our lanes,
Coming down at evening, their arms full
Of cowslips, moon daisies, whinberries, nuts,
      All fruits of the sliding seasons,
And the enormous experience of the mountain

That I who loved it did not understand.
In the summer, dust filled our winter ruts
With a level softness, and children walked
At evening through golden curtains scuffed
      From the road by their trailing feet.
They would drink tiredly at our wall, talking

Softly, leaning, their sleepy faces warm for home.
We would see them murmur slowly through our stiff
Gate, their shy heads gilded by the last sun.
One by one we would gather up the used jugs,
      The glasses. We would pour away
A little water. It would lie on the thick dust, gleaming.

Ransoms

(for Edward Thomas)

What the white ransoms did was to wipe away
The dry irritation of a journey half across
England. In the warm tiredness of dusk they lay
Like moonlight fallen clean onto the grass,

And I could not pass them. I wound
Down the window for them and for the still
Falling dark to come in as they would,
And then remembered that this was your hill,

Your precipitous beeches, your wild garlic.
I thought of you walking up from your house
And your heartbreaking garden, melancholy
Anger sending you into this kinder darkness,

And the shining ransoms bathing the path
With pure moonlight. I have my small despair
And would not want your sadness; your truth,
Your tragic honesty, are what I know you for.

I think of a low house upon a hill,
Its door closed now even to the hushing wind
The tall grass bends to, and all the while
The far-off salmon river without sound

Runs on below; but if this vision should
Be yours or mine I do not know. Pungent
And clean the smell of ransoms from the wood,
And I am refreshed. It was not my intent

To stop on a solitary road, the night colder,
Talking to a dead man, fifty years dead,
But as I flick the key, hear the engine purr,
Drive slowly down the hill, I'm comforted.

The white, star-shaped flowers of the Wood Garlic, *Allium ursinum Liliaceae*, are usually known as 'Ramsons'; but W. Keble Martin, in *The Concise British Flora in Colour*, (Ebury Press and Michael Joseph, 1965), calls them *Ransoms*. They grow profusely from April to June in the beech hangers above Edward Thomas's house outside Petersfield. Obviously, in the context of the poem, *Ransoms* means much more than the usual name.

Now the House Sleeps

Now the house sleeps among its trees,
Those charcoal scratches on the sky's
Good morning, and I walk the lane
That all night long has quietly gone
Down the cold hill, and quietly up
Until it reached that darkened top
Where the shrill light of a short day
Begins again the frozen glow

Of winter dawn. I contemplate
The wealth of day that has to wait
The recognition of my eye.
Reality is what we see,
Or what my senses all achieve;
What they believe, so I believe.
Around, the ring of hills wears light
Of morning like a steel helmet

And below them, in the brown
Cleansing of its floods, runs down
The brawling river. Now the owl,
That all night held its floating call
Over the terrified hedges, climbs
In clumsy blindness to the elm's
Black safety, there flops down,
A comfortable, daylight clown;

And little animals of night
Retire as silent as the light
To sleeping darkness. Closing the door,
I leave the white fields desert for
The loss of my descriptive eye.
The sunlit measures of the day
Are unregarded. I cut bread,
Knowing the world untenanted.

And yet, although my sight must stop
At the solid wall, a world builds up,
Feature by feature, root by root,
The soft advance of fields, daylight
Reaching west in the turn of life,
Personal, created world, half
Ignorant, half understood. And I
Complete from faulty memory

And partial complexities of sense
Those images of experience
That make approximate rivers move
Through the wrong world in which I live,
Or chart a neat uncertainty
Down major roads to Nowhere City;
But at the edge of what I know
The massed, appalling forests grow.

Through the long night the rough trucks grind
The highways, gears ripping blind,
Headlights awash on the tarmac;
All night long metallic traffic,
Racks of concrete, rams of girders,
Heavy oppression of cities
Forced by a crude growling. Yet all
Are Plato's shadows on the wall,

Noises drifting among shadows,
Shadows dying among echoes,
While clear eternities of light
Shine somewhere on the perfect world
We cannot know. My shadowed field
Lies in its flawed morning, and dirt
Falls in the slow ditches. Sunrise,
And the house wakes among its trees.

Postcards from Wales

Whenever I think of Wales, I hear the voices
Of children calling, and the world shrinks to the span
Of a dozen hills. As I wander to sleep
The water voices of the streams begin.

> *Green air, the truthful winds shall sing you*
> *Over the lean hill and the melancholy*
> *Valley of childhood.*

We swam free rivers that our tongues resembled,
We lit the summer dark with lazy fire
At the waterside. And when silence fell
It was not passing time we grew to hear,

> *Winter. The blind lake turns its solid*
> *Eye to the snowcloud. In the village*
> *The doors are fast, the chimneys fat with coalsmoke*

But the world changing, the tall hills tumbling,
The universe of terraces waning small.
Beyond brief rivers we heard the urgent sea
Knock to come in. It was a miracle

> *The spent salmon drops tail first to the sea.*
> *His lank sides heave. His exhausted eye*
> *Turns away for another year.*

Of our own discovering. Whenever I think of Wales,
I think of my leaving, the farewell valleys letting go
And the quick voices falling far behind in the dust
Off the dry tips. And I think of returning, too,

> *Cae Gwair is spotted with orchises;*
> *The earth, finding its own rich heat,*
> *Releases it in little purple columns.*

On some afternoon warm and loving, to a handful
Of fields by Teifi river and a cottage blind
With waiting. I know those rough, wind-turning
Walls were made in childhood, I know my mind

> *In September the cold ponies*
> *Return from the high moor. They kick*
> *Down the tottering stones and relish the gardens.*

Invents the long, immaculate weather of a year
Unpredictable as truth. But the river's voice
Is forever filling the valley, filling it,
And remembered voices are underneath my windows.

Stones

On the flat of the earth lie
Stones, their eyes turned
To earth's centre, always.
If you throw them they fly
Grudgingly, measuring your arm's
Weak curve before homing
To a place they know.

Digging, we may jostle
Stones with our thin tines
Into stumbling activity.
Small ones move most.
When we turn from them
They grumble to a still place.
It can take a month to grate

That one inch. Watch how stones
Clutter together on hills
And beaches, settling heavily
In unremarkable patterns.

A single stone can vanish
In a black night, making
Someone bury it in water.

We can polish some;
Onyx, perhaps, chalcedony,
Jasper and quartzite from
The edges of hard land.
But we do not alter them.
Once in a million years
Their stone hearts lurch.

Merman

(for Kit Barker)

When I first came to the air I fell
Through its empty thickets. Dry
Land attacked me, and I lay
With my skin in grit, drily.
The drab, sudden weight of my
Gagging flesh dragged me, would pull

Me down. Nor would my swimming
Bones erect me. It was a grunting
Crawl I moved at. There was not need
For the rough cords they locked me in.
Later, in the animal compound, pooled
In a small dead water of their making,

I hid my staring sex, and wept.
As my stale gills crumbled
Like bread, and slow lungs held
Air with a regular comfort,
I learned to prod locked bones
To a jolt of walking. Their sounds

Came last to my mouth
And were useful for freedom.
I who had been a sad monster
In the kept zoo of their fear
Live at equal liberty with
Them now. At dark I come

From watching the tame harbour
Where nudged ships depart,
And in my tideless cell I dream
The great seas break far over me,
Silent; and I dream I drift
In upright seagrowth, in the living water.

A Girl's Song

Early one morning
As I went out walking
I saw the young sailor
Go fresh through the fields.
His eye was as blue as
The sky up above us
And clean was his skin
As the colour of shells.

O where are you going,
Young sailor, so early?
And may I come with you
A step as you go?
He looked with his eye
And I saw the deep sea-tombs,
He opened his mouth
And I heard the sea roar.

And limp on his head
Lay his hair green as sea-grass
And scrubbed were his bones
By the inching of sand.
The long tides enfolded
The lines of his body
And slow corals grow
At the stretch of his hand.

I look from my window
In the first light of morning
And I look from my door
At the dark of the day,
But all that I see are
The fields flat and empty
And the black road run down
To Cardigan town.

Fishing the Teifi

Left bank and right,
I've fished this water since first light,
Pitching my early spinners
Into the river's mirrors,
Feeling the hook sink
Minutely, then I'd check, and bring it to the bank.

It was enough at first
To know the thrown perfection of each cast,
My eight-foot, fibreglass flinger
Growing from my hand, a finger
To set exactly down
My teal and black, mallard and claret, or coachman.

But I've had nothing on
All morning nor the longer afternoon.
For all his hunched attention
The empty heron's flown,
And now the soft-whistling otter
Glides his long belly into the blackening water.

From the bleak dark the hiss
Of a harsh wind turns my face
Down like a sheet, telling me to go.
But sleep tonight I know
Will not shut out this river, nor the gleam
Of big fish, sliding up to hook onto my dream.

The One Leaf

An oak leaf fell from the tree
Into my hand almost, so I kept it.
First in my fingers, very carefully,
Because it was mine. I wiped it,
Put it on my desk, near the typewriter.
Last autumn there were oak leaves falling everywhere.

I could have chosen from so many.
It lay there months, turning browner,
Before I no longer saw it. Now
Here it is again, an old letter
From plenty. From where I stand
This is the one leaf, in the cold house, on the cold ground.

It's Somebody's Birthday

This birthday man
Rises from my hot bed
Into his mirror.
When I groan
Out of his crumpled head
He prods my dewlap with a jeering finger.

Behind his eyes
Lie the slim silver boys
Called by my name.
No blind surprise
Nor moving without noise
Shall ever startle them inside that frame.

To my round skin
He will remain flat true,
Warning for warning.
I pull my stomach in,
March a hard step or two,
Shut loud the bathroom door, murder his morning.

Drummer Evans

There was a great elm in Drummer Evans's garden.
Half of his house it kept in daylight shadow; all summer
A chaffinch sang in its highest branches, swinging
In an invisible cage its music was so local.
Drummer dribbled it crumbs from his fingers
As he sat on a log, his back to the elm trunk,
One slow leg straight before him, and his yellow hand,
His fingers, playing intricate patterns on his other knee.
He was small, his eyes looked upward always.

His face was mild and ivory, composed and smooth.
He wore a black suit and a very wide hat and he called
All women Mrs Jones, because it was easier.
I went to him Tuesdays and Saturdays for lessons.

My kettle-drum set on its three-legged stand,
He would flick its resonance with a finger and say,
'Now boy, two with each hand, away you go; and
Don't let the drumstick tamp'. Tamp was a word for bounce,
We always used it. Away I'd go, two with each hand,
Back of the wrists to the skin, sticks held lightly,
And clumsily double beat with each hack fist,
Tap-tap, tap-tap, tap-tap, until that unskilled knock
Snarled in my tired arms and stuttered out.
I don't remember getting any better, but he'd nod,
Still for a while his drumming hand, and smile,
And say, 'Again'.
          When I could play no more he'd take the sticks
And give to my stubborn drum a pliant eloquence.
I'd leave then. The bird was nearly always singing.
It never rained in Drummer Evans's garden.

Because I knew that I would never make
On an echoing hull those perfect measures
Heard in my head as I marched at the head of armies
Or rattling between the beat of my running heels,
I left the Drummer.
               It was an idle sun
Recalled his garden, and an unclaimed bird
Singing from a thorn his tame bird's song
That brought the old man back,
Martial hands parading and muttering.
I went by the river's edge and stone bridge
To his thundering cottage.

For the air for half a mile was rhythmical thunder.
Roll after roll of exact, reverberant challenge,
The flames of history unfurled their names from my books,
Agincourt, Malplaquet, Waterloo, Corunna,

And I reached at a gasp the Drummer's beleaguered garden
Ringed by standing friends at the rim of his anger,
He stood strapped for war from the fury of their kindness,
Striking his sharp refusal of all pity
The women offered. 'Come on,' they called,
                              'Ah, come on Mr Evans.'
But he swept them away with the glory of his drumfire,
Hands flying high in volleys of retaliation.
The tree held its sunlight like a flag of honour
And helpless, uniformed men spoke out to him softly;
But his side-drum returned defiance for this old man
Whose proud skill told us he was Drummer Evans,
No common mister to be hauled to the Poorhouse.

Winter Song

Over the bluff hills
At the day's end
The diffident snow
Swirls before dropping

Blow wind, blow
That we may see
Your smooth body

The humble snow
Is waiting for darkness
So its soft light
Can muffle the hills

Blow wind, blow
The copse will be silent
The black trees empty

At the day's end
The small snow is scurrying
White bees in the moon
And the flying wind

Blow wind
Over the cold hills
For the moon is voiceless

Grass

I walk on grass more often
Than most men. Something in me
Still values wealth as a wide field
With blades locked close enough
To keep soil out of mind. It is a test
Of grass when I push a foot
Hard on its green spring. The high pastures
I mean, open to the unfenced wind,
Bitten by sheep.

                Go into Hereford,
My grandfather said, (his dwarf
Grass was scarce as emeralds,
The wet peat crept brown into his happiness),
In Hereford the grass is up to your waist.
We could not gather such unthinkable richness,
We stared over the scraped hill to luscious England.

Behind us the spun brook whitened
On boulders, and rolled, a slow thread
On the eyes, to bubbling pebbles.

I have been in wet grass up to the waist,
In loaded summer, on heavy summer mornings,
And when I came away my clothes, my shoes,
My hair even, were full of hard seeds
Of abundant grass. Brushes would not remove them.

Winters, I know grass is alive
In quiet ditches, in moist, secret places
Warmed by the two-hour sun. And as the year
Turns gently for more light,
Viridian grass moves out to lie in circles,
Live wreaths for the dying winter.

Soon roots of couch-grass,
Sly, white, exploratory, will lie
Bare to my spade. Smooth and pliable,
Their sleek heads harder
And more durable than granite.
It is worth fighting against grass.

Two Men

1. *Billy Price*

He would open the loft early
And his soft-voiced flock
Turned in the morning
Like a bird with a hundred wings.

On workless days he would sing
Freely, and girls in neighbouring
Backyards applauded him
With joined choruses and the frankness of their smiles.

At evening he would signal in his pigeons.
When I began to whistle I learned this call;
A ladder of falling notes across the bars as the birds
Folded themselves home.

2. *John Williams*

His father had drunk away many acres
And a whole flock of mountain sheep.
He had been tall, red-bearded, strong as legend,
Ridden to market on a pony much too small,

But John Williams was deliberately not like this.
Mild and silver from his youth,
He had refused even to grow very much.
At fourteen I was inches over his eighty years.

The day he was eighty we leaned on his gate
And he told me of his fading eyes.
There was a signpost on the horizon opposite
He could scarcely see. Staring at that far

Mountain-edge, I could see only the dissolving
Motes of the air. But he had turned away.
'When you are old,' he said, 'when you are old
You know where all the fingerposts are.'

Dog

On a field like a green roof
Pitched by the sea wind
A patch of uncertain sheep
Each poised on pointed hoof
Ready for running
Stare at the coiled bitch
Alert for their turning

And stamp as she sidles
And freezes. They pick
At the steep field, they back,
Disturbing the nervous edge
Of their fleecy circle.
Slowly the bitch inches
And with a rush

Channels the stunned run.
They stream in a prim file
Through the one marked gap
In the leaning hedge,
And Fan, tongue sideways lolling
Ushers them softly through.
Adrift on the stiff hill

The cold shepherd does not even watch them.

Space Miner

(for Robert Morgan)

His face was a map of traces where veins
Had exploded bleeding in atmospheres too
Frail to hold that life, and scar tissue
Hung soft as pads where his cheekbones shone
Under the skin when he was young.
He had worked deep seams where encrusted ore,
Too tight for his diamond drill, had ripped
Strips from his flesh. Dust from a thousand metals
Silted his lungs and softened the strength
Of his muscles. He had worked the treasuries
Of many near stars, but now he stood on the moving
Pavement reserved for cripples who had served well.
The joints of his hands were dry and useless
Under the cold gloves issued by the government.

Before they brought his sleep in a little capsule
He would look through the hospital window
At the ships of young men bursting into space.
For this to happen he had worked till his body broke.
Now they flew to the farthest worlds in the universe;
Mars, Eldorado, Mercury, Earth, Saturn.

The Dead

(after the Welsh of Gwenallt, 1899-1968)

Reaching fifty, a man has time to recognise
His ordinary humanity, the common echoes
In his own voice. And I think with compassion
Of the graves of friends who died. When I was young,

Riding the summer on a bike from the scrap-yard,
Kicking Wales to victory with all I could afford —
A pig's bladder — how could I have known
That two of my friends would suffer the torn

Agony of slimy death from a rotten lung,
Red spittle letting their weakening
Living into a bucket? They were our neighbours,
Lived next door. We called them the Martyrs

Because they came from Merthyr Tydfil, that
Town of furnaces. Whenever I thought
I'd laugh, a cough ripped over the wall,
Scraping my ribs with cinders. It was all

Done at last, and I crept in to look,
Over the coffin's edge and the black
Rim of the Bible, at the dry flesh free
Of breath, too young for the cemetery.

And I protest at such death without dignity,
Death brutally invoked, death from the factory,
Immature death, blind death, death which mourning
Does not comfort, without tears. I bring

From my mind a small house huge with death,
Where heavy women cut sticks, deal with
The fires, the laborious garden, their little
Money dissolving in the hand. Terrible

Are the blasphemous wars and savageries I
Have lived through, animal cruelty
Loose like a flame through the whole world;
Yet here on Flower Sunday, in a soiled

Acre of graves, I lay down my gasping roses
And lilies pale as ice as one who knows
Nothing certain, nothing; unless it is
My own small place and people, agony and sacrifice.

Owls

The owls are flying. From hedge to hedge
Their deep-mouthed voices call the fields
Of England, stretching north and north,
To a sibilant hunt above ditches;
And small crawlers, bent in crevices, yield
Juice of their threaded veins, with

A small kernel of bones. It was earlier
I walked the lace of the sea at this south
Edge, walked froths of the fallen moon
Bare-legged in the autumn water
So cold it set my feet like stones
In its inches, and I feel on breath

And ankles the touch of the charged sea
Since. I saw in my lifting eyes the flat
Of this one country, north stretching,
And north. I saw its hills, the public light
Of its cities, and every blatant tree
Burning, with assembled autumn burning.

I know the same sun, in a turn
Of earth, will bring morning, grey
As gulls or mice to us. And I know
In my troubled night the owls fly
Over us, wings wide as England,
And their voices will never go away.

October in the Lane

October in the lane, and the thin harebells,
Ghosts of their deep Augusts, pine in the hedges.
Puffed leaves thicken the crawling ditches
And tired wasps labour in the air,

Heavy with dying. Our trees prepare
The black calligraphies of winter, we strip
Our fields for the frost fire. Now roses drop
From the wall their falls of petals

And cheat my eyes with snowflakes. Smells
Of marauding weather come coldly in with the dark.
I remember a spring of snow that fell without mark
On my head and white hurry as I thudded for home

And we laughed to see how soon I became,
In a falling minute, a seven year old, white-haired man.
In the kitchen mirror I watched the quick years run
From the warm, and I wiped from my head

The unready white my April time pretended.
So many weathers have spread their tempers near me
That empty winters stretch behind my mirror
And the keenest razor will not shift their snowfalls.

A True Death

(for Vernon Watkins 1906-1967)

When summer is dead, when evening
October is dying, the pendulum
Heart falters, and the firm
Blood hangs its drops in a swing
Of stone. Laughing, we catch breath
Again. But his was the true death

Our rehearsals imitate. I lived
On the charred hills where industrial
Fires for a hundred years had grieved
All things growing. On still,
On the stillest days, a burnish
Of sea glinted at the world's edge

And died with the sun. There
Were twenty miles of Wales between
My streams and the water lore
He knew. He watched the green
Passages of the sea, how it rides
The changing, unchanging roads

Of its hollowing power. Caves
From his flooded cliffs called to him,
Dunes with their harsh grasses
Sang, the river-mouths spoke of home
In Carmarthen hills. Small stones
Rang like bells, touching his hands.

Last year we sat in his garden,
Quietly, in new wooden chairs,
Grasshoppers rasped on the hot lawn.
Shadows gathered at his shoulders
As he spoke of the little tormentil,
Tenacious flower; growing there still.

Old Voices

First the one bell, heavy, behind it
Centuries of controlled certainty, swung
With an enormous sound past
The kneeling city; it is the first
Heard stone in an architecture of ringing.
And sung in at built intervals, at
The joint of locked structure, the voice
Of the second bell. The foundation is

Set on unimpeded air. An age
Of cut stone and iron — those old
Technologies — has its immense medieval
Tongues bellowing again. Now all
The small bells filigree and stretch
A long nave in the ear and a pulled
Spire of sailing clamour. Resonant
Cathedrals of listening are launched

On the open day. But bells are not
Peaceful; are arrogant with the complete
World of their origin. Think, imagine,
In the clack of swords they began,
Short on their own shields the flat beat
Struck, so that erratic courage set
Hard in the metal; then the high edge,
Turning in the urgency of the charge,

Rang through the heads of wives
At their keen mourning. Hacking the bent
Angles of helmets, rough blades cracked again
The wombs that bore these splintered heads
In their early down. From such sounds,
From the held quiet after, the brazen
Complexities of the loud tower grew.
There was time for the patterns of victory,

And space on the fat plains of grain
For building of flawless bells. The lost
In their slate hills had tongues only,
Grew old in the slow labour
Of changing myths. Through the mist
Of altering voices their stories spun,
Through generations of telling. Spiral
Images from the belfries, the metal

Confections of chiming, are not
For the mountains. Old men tell
Of an impermanent peace, a fragile
Faith is passed through narrative
Villages in syllables of live
Whispers. Foolish now to regret
Centuries of locked exile. It happened.
We have heads full of easy legend

And elegies like the cold sun
Of treeless autumn. I carry
Such tunes in my head like the thin
Silence the bells hang in. But from
These reaching fields my surnamed
Fathers came, the great cathedrals
Counted them. I walk their lanes,
My shoes cover the concave stones

Worn by their slow tolling.
If I speak with the quick brooks
Of the permanent hills, in my saying
See hordes of the dark tribes stand,
Their faces hidden, my hand
In its perfect glove of skin holds
Other ghosts. We step the streets
Uneasily, disturbed by bells.

Mountains Polecats Pheasants

Stone and Fern

It is not that the sea lanes
Are too long, nor that I am not
Tempted by the birds' sightless

Roads, but that I have listened
Always to the voice of the stone,
Saying: Sit still, answer, say

Who you are. And I have answered
Always with the rooted fern,
Saying: We are the dying seed.

Barn Owl

Ernie Morgan found him, a small
Fur mitten inexplicably upright,
And hissing like a treble kettle
Beneath the tree he'd fallen from.
His bright eye frightened Ernie,
Who popped a rusty bucket over him
And ran for us. We kept him
In a backyard shed, perched
On the rung of a broken deck-chair,
Its canvas faded to his down's biscuit.
Men from the pits, their own childhood
Spent waste in the crippling earth,
Held him gently, brought him mice
From the wealth of our riddled tenements,
Saw that we understood his tenderness,
His tiny body under its puffed quilt,
Then left us alone. We called him Snowy.

He was never clumsy. He flew
From the first like a skilled moth,
Sifting the air with feathers,
Floating it softly to the place he wanted.
At dusk he'd stir, preen, stand
At the window-ledge, fly. It was
A catching of the heart to see him go.
Six months we kept him, saw him
Grow beautiful in a way each thought
His own knowledge. One afternoon, home
With pretended illness, I watched him
Leave. It was daylight. He lifted slowly
Over the Hughes's roof, his cream face calm,
And never came back. I saw this;
And tell it for the first time,
Having wanted to keep his mystery.

And would not say it now, but that
This morning, walking in Slindon woods
Before the sun, I found a barn owl
Dead in the rusty bracken.
He was not clumsy in his death,
His wings folded decently to him,
His plumes, unruffled orange,
Bore flawlessly their delicate patterning.
With a stick I turned him, not
Wishing to touch his feathery stiffness.
There was neither blood nor wound on him,
But for the savaged foot a scavenger
Had ripped. I saw the sinews.
I could have skewered them out
Like a common fowl's. Moving away
I was oppressed by him, thinking
Confusedly that down the generations
Of air this death was Snowy's
Emblematic messenger, that I should know
The meaning of it, the dead barn owl.

At Usk

On a cold day, in the church-
yard, between the gate and
the west door's unlocked arch,

lay the flat stone. It was
anonymous. It might have
gained by chance its grace

of simple effigy, round
eyeless head, rough torso,
a hint of sleeping child

in its stillness; a brown
stone of Monmouthshire
shaped and polished by rain.

A child was kneeling there,
absorbed, concentrating,
measuring with happy care

on the cold of breast
and throat her offering
of snowdrop and crocus.

She matched the flowers,
placed them on the stone
child with her red fingers,

and then ran off to some
warm house in the town.
Now on the stone a film

of winter sap sticks the
limp stalks, but it is
the child at home that I

think of as I walk quickly
through God's still acre.
Her gifts delight me, and I

am leaving Usk, moving
towards the M4, clearly
right to praise the living.

A Glass Window, In Memory of Edward Thomas, At Eastbury Church

The road lay in moistening valleys, lanes
Awash with evening, expensive racehorses
Put to bed in pastures under the elms.
I was disappointed. Something in me turns

Urchin at so much formality, such pastoral
Harmony. I grumble for rock outcrops,
In filed, rasping country. The church drips
Gently, in perfect English, and we all

Troop in, see the lit window, smile, and look
Again; shake out wet coats. Under your name
The images of village, hill and home,
And crystal England stands against the dark.

The path cut in the pane most worries me,
Coming from nowhere, moving into nowhere.
Is it the road to the land no traveller
Tells of? I turn away, knowing it is, for me,

That sullen lane leading you out of sight,
In darkening France, the road taken.
Suddenly I feel the known world shaken
By gunfire, by glass breaking. In comes the night.

His Last Autumn

(for Andrew Young, 1885-1971)

He had never known such an autumn.
At his slow feet were apples
Redder than sun, and small flowers,
Their names no longer thought of,

Grew afresh in his recovered innocence.
His eyes had taken colour of the speedwell.
Looking at the sea, he felt its
Lifting pull as he dived, years deep,

Where slant light picked the rocks
With brilliants. It was the distant
Road of his boyhood we drove along
On sunny afternoons, it was the laid

Dust of his past that rose beneath
Our wheels. Tranquilly the weather
Lingered, warm day after warm day.
He was dead when the cold weather came.

The Yew Tree Above the Grave of Dafydd ap Gwilym

(after the Welsh of Gruffudd Gryg, fl. 1357-1370)

A tree grows at the wall
Of Ystrad Fflur, the great hall.
God's grace to it, for it is blessed
To be the house of Dafydd,
And his own spent beauty
Dafydd gives to the yew tree.

91

Even before you grew
Dafydd said this of you:
You were named for his home,
Death's keep against storm,
Against blizzard, hard wind;
As once birches were kind
In the snows of his manhood.
Now he lives in your root and wood.

Beneath, you hold the grave
Of him I could not save.
He was the world's angel-swarm
Himself, when he was warm,
And loss of his wise voice
Took brightness from Dyddgu's face.

He made all things grow for her,
Rich crops and clover.
Yew tree, it's your turn
To show how well you mourn.
Gently guard his tomb-stone,
Weep, like a maid, alone;
With your roots like a tripod
Take care you never tread
One step from his head.

And yew tree, for your care,
Goats shall not soil or tear
The house of your lord.
Fire you can discard,
And loss from carpenter
And stripping cobbler.
True love won't carve a name
On the bark of your frame,
Nor shall woodman bend
For fear of punishment
To axe through the boughs
Of my friend's green house.

Green, Dafydd, grows your roof,
Like the freshness of love.

The Green Bridge

What shall we write about, in
Wales, where the concentration
Camps are a thousand years old,

And some of our own making?
I live in England, seem English,
Until my voice and wider

Eloquence betray me: then
I am a discovered alien.
I walk on Teifi banks, through

Snowdrops left us by the Romans,
Watching the river pour to death
In the sea, the February sea

Where Irish wailing thinly rides
The water. I have a blood group
Common only in Carmarthenshire.

The Wales I walk is a green bridge
To death — not yet, please God —
On which I am not lonely;

But journey on, thinking of
The dead Irish; hearing, far off,
The owners of Africa calling for freedom.

Burning the Bracken

When summer stopped, and the last
Lit cloud blazed tawny cumulus
Above the hills, it was the bracken

Answered; its still crests
Contained an autumn's burning.
Then, on an afternoon of promised

Cold, true flames ripped
The ferns. Hurrying fire, low
And pale in the sun, ran

Glittering through them. As
Night fell, the brindle
Flambeaux, full of chattering

We were too far to hear, leapt
To the children's singing.
'Fire on the mountain,' we

Chanted, who went to bed warmed
By joy. But I would know that fires
Die, that the cold sky holds

Uneasily the fronds and floating
Twigs of broken soot, letting
Them fall, fall now, soft

As darkness on this white page.

Mountains Polecats Pheasants

I have seen these hills closed
By impassive winter, and stood,
Banging my arms, on the last
Cold yard of road before snow
Came down on memory, the way

Strange as Asia. In summer,
Loss of the travelled sun drops
A bulk of mountain into shadow
Deep enough to lose a town in,
And scared cars, smaller, run

For the lit valleys. I thought
The mountains safe in my mind
From all revelation, but
Had never before driven late
Their cleft passes. Midnight

Had left the road as I climbed
The foothills, the car slotted
Behind headlights and the warmed
Engine humming at gradients
Above the farms. Fenceless

The ponies slept, their fetlocks
Still, their wild skulls fallen
To stone. It was a dark
Palpable as ice on those
Stone ranges. On a blunt rise,

Where the wind scorched black
The stump hawthorns and hedge
Grass bent thick in the shock
Of wind, I saw in my lights
Such tiny brilliances. Not cats',

Not foxes' eyes shone colder.
Cutting the engine, I softened
Downroad to where they were:
Polecats, the mother stiff
With instinct, her emeralds of

Sight full on my pointing;
Her five young, caught
In a lesson of hunting.
Fear moved her, sliding her
Flat as oil and under

The light; but her innocents
Stayed, weaving their baby heads.
They mewed, their sweet throats
Tame as milk. Their gentling
Cries showed me their kindling,

Blind in a hard nest under
The piled rocks. I knew the slit
Of their eyes against the thunder
Of light. I wished for them
A lenient dark and safe home.

Last year, in true daylight,
At a faultless eighty on
Other roads, it was soft
Death I passed. A bag, burst
Cushion, cracked feathers drift-

ing after smash, the hen
Pheasant lay. There was no
Terror in that sight. When
She was puffed to one side
In a bundle of snapped

Shafts, she lay roundly where
She fell. The slow blood
Failed to mark the air
For her, but in the fallen
Wreaths of her plumes ran

Her dozen chicks, no more
Than hours after hatching.
I could not catch them, nor
Could I harry them to safe
Hiding before rough

Death wiped their brief
Smudges under the wheels
Of cars. The stuff of
The roads, oil, grit, fine
Dust, absorbed their stain.

There was nothing to show for them,
Though they came from the perfect
Eggs this mother alone could form.
When she died, feathers hung
A week in the hedge, turning

Black in the hot exhausts.
I know that my polecats
Are old now in the deaths
Of their needed victims,
I know there are cold times.

When the fields whistle
In fear of them, the grass
Thickens as they ripple
Through, tearing murder. Yet
I would have had them meet,

Polecats and pheasants, on
Their common hills. I would
Have had them live, and
In a night more terrible
Than the terrible fall

Of shadow or winter over
These mountains I close again,
Let the truth turn clear
For them, the last whimper
Of it, true hunted, true hunter.

Deerhound

There are no deerhounds in Wales —
Or perhaps one; in Cardiff, loping
On an elegant lead in Llandaff Fields,
Exotic in Queen Street, posing
For photographs. But there are
No true deerhounds. Our fat corgis
Sit irritably in English country houses,
Our loyal collies starve
Behind the doors of roadless farms.

We parade our terriers. Square
And bristling, the brisk wire-
Haired fox terrier, the Welsh terrier
Indigenous black and tan, thin
Scars on head and legs, like a collier,
We like these dogs. I knew one
Curl herself over a drunk man's heart,
On a moor filling with blizzard.
They grin at death with their teeth.

I would have a deerhound coloured
Slippery as charcoal, running
Tactfully at the edge of eyesight,
Soft as dust after his great quarry.
Once, back of the ruined hills, I saw
A fabulous hare living on grass
Too small for sheep, thrusting,
Through coal-spoil. He leapt
In my sleep for months.

With such small deer my hound
Would not soil his slobber.
In darkness, on the edge of terror,
He would run loose, he would run loose and
Noiseless. Black as nightfur, kicking
Into the black, what antlered
Game he would rip at, what
Terrible beasts drag back
Alive for my keeping.

The Thrush Singing

(from the Welsh of Dafydd ap Gwilym, fl. 1320-1370)

Strong was the art and onrush
Of a flecked singer, the thrush
Who from the tree's height sprang
His unfettered singing.
Listen, oh let your ear fill!
No voice for the sorrowful,
But loud for the proud boy
And girl in early May
He whistles out a love-note
With every pulse of his throat.

Brook-clear, carol-call, day-bright,
Music lucid as light
He sang again and again,
Of happiness without pain,
Yesterday, all yesterday,
While I beneath a birch lay.

His reverend feathers on,
He reads the morning lesson
Exultant from his thicket:
He sets morning alight.
Hill-seer, light's interpreter,
Love's poet of leafy summer,
He sings as his privilege
Every song of the stream's edge,
Every soft, honey sonnet,
Every organ throb below it,
Spendthrift of his nature's art
To capture a girl's heart.
He preaches, bidding us come
To Ovid's flawless kingdom,
This bird, perfect priest of
May, headlong voice of love.

Lovers meet at his birch-tree
And he offers them freely
The deep wealth of his passion.
Or he'll sing where he's hidden
In a tangle of hazel —
Cloister-trees and bird-angel —
Songs lost by Heaven's fallen,
Songs he makes from love alone.

Moondaisies

They open from a hard involucre,
Stand about two feet high, are
Rayed and arrayed in white: summer
Flowers, whitest in hot weather.

They grip the soil at hedgesides,
Opening their spotless moons above
What grass they live in. Children love
Them. They are more candid than any words.

Grow best in railway cuttings, deep
Bees among their petals, but grow
Anywhere; radiant, stubborn, cut low
By winter; common as hope.

July the Seventh

Drugged all day, the summer
Flagged in its heat, brutal
Weather sullen as brass.
There was no comfort in darkness.
Hotter than breath we lay

On beds too warm for moving,
Near open windows. Full of
Spaces the house was, walls
Fretting for a brisk air.
A door slammed flat in its

Loud frame, banging us awake.
Wind was bringing in the storm.
Quick switches of whipped light
Flicked the rooftops, made shadowless
The ends of rooms. The stopped clock

Marked the lightning. I got up
Heavily, shut the house against
Thunder. Rain was a long time
Coming, then sparse drops, stinging
Like metal, hit the bricks, the hot

Pavements. When it sweetened
To plenty, the streets tamed it,
Flowed it in pipes and conduits,
Channelled it underground through
Stony runnels. The rain brought

So faint a smell of hay I searched
My mind for it, thinking it memory.
I lay freshly awake on the cool sheets,
Hearing the storm. Somewhere, far off,
Cut grass lay in files, the hay spoiling.

Beachmaster

His mother, from the loving sea
Lurching, found him by smell,
Though the nursery beach
Was thick with milk, and other
Blubber. Her comfort was all
Tacky liquid and the touch

Of nuzzle and rubbery flipper.
Weak and thin at first, he was
Afraid of water. But grew
Lusty, casting in plump sleep
His long, white, birthday fur.
In a ring it lay. He was

Left miniature sleek seal.
After three weeks she abandoned
Him, the call of heavy bull
In the sexual tide and swell
Being too much, though he moaned
With his pup's silk mouth the whole

Of a day. That night he snarled
At the spray and set off.
In ten weeks such a pup, in
Its first green diving of
The seaways, untaught, alone
In bottle-coloured water,

Swam six hundred miles, to Spain.
That was not my pup, though he
Savaged fast shoals in places
Far away, and dragged his growing
Awkwardly over other beaches.
This is his country, where young

Cows come out to call him home
And meadows of the sea swing
Miles deep under him. Here
He first fought, nostrils popping
In muscled water, in fury
Of instinct, for a territory.

He keeps ward off shore, armour
Of scar thickening shoulder
And neck; hulk bull, upright
In lull. Nobody sees him eat.
On the loud beach, his sons, small,
Weak, wait for white fur to fall.

Shadows

(for John Ormond)

In the night world, it was
The river was black.
Not reeds at the water's
Edge, streaked with darkness,
Not the dim coldness, back
Under the trees, were black.

It was the river. And
He lay in his smooth pool,
Slack in it, blind
In it, fanning the sand
Under him, with his tail.
He did not hear at all

Quick whispers on the bank,
Nor the furtive launching
From the brink
Of the river. His roof broke
In a small furrow along
The bend, in the swing

Of the current. He did
Not know. He lay safe
In his size, the cold
Strength that none could
Be stronger. With a flick of
His neck he could rip off

The cheap lures cast for him,
He could bull the water
Until it boiled after him,
Even out of heavy calm,
Even out of warm summer
Glaze, with his bludgeoning shoulder.

But now he lay in the balm
Tide, under the boat sailed
Secretly to kill him,
And he did not know. For him
Alone the darkness held
Its breath over river and field.

When the light slashed
The water, white torch
Pointed at him, lanced
At him, he held clenched
Against fright in the touch
Of light. He did not flinch

From lick of light, the sun
Itself in the healthy day
Did not disturb him when
He rolled in his weight down
Bending falls. But now
It was the shadow

Of his fear hung under
Him, black, ominous, pressed
Flat against gravel. Whether
The mincing river
Trembled it, or greed
Quivered the hawk boat,

He knew in his skin
The hunger of its waiting.
And he turned quietly in
From the edge of light, watching
It turn with him, cling
To him; and it ran

Behind him and under
Him as he ran
From the closing floor

Of the river.
His shadow ran
As close as the pain

Of his terror, and now
He swam furiously from
It, up, from it, away
From it, into
The clear light of freedom.
And the murderous gaff saved him.

And our faces stared red,
Reflecting
His gashed blood.
The shadow of his killing,
Sunk under mortal stain,
Waits other lights, other salmon.

In October

Moving into fall, I give my body rest
After heady summer. The hills turn early blue,
                    The rivers are rising.

Yesterday, winds from the untempered north
Put me shutting windows. At night I closed my eyes
                    On the last of summer.

I have set the fire, collecting the slight
Twigs. Spent as leaves, I watch my fallen hands,
                    The bark hardening.

Winter Birds

Most mornings now they're there,
Humped on the chestnut fence
Awaiting the regular hour
That brings me out of the shower,
Warm, pulling on my pants,
Enjoying a last yawn.
They might have been there since dawn,

And have been for all I know.
So I crumble up their bread
As a famished one or two
Hop down on to the snow —
Thrushes, all bold eye
And cream and coffee feather.
How they confront the weather!

It is habit, I suppose,
That brings these birds to wait,
And the natures that they all
So variously inherit
Show up as they strut and eat —
These starlings now, they call
Their friends to share the meal.

And when all seems to have gone
An elegant wagtail comes,
Turning his slender neck
And precise, selective beak
To feed on specks so small
They seem not there at all.
He eats the crumbs of crumbs.

But the harsh, predatory,
Scavenging, black-headed gulls
Uncertainly wheel and call,
Or balefully sit in the field.

Though fiercely hunger pulls
They will not come for the bread
And fly at the lift of my head.

But it is the gulls I hear
As I take the car down the road,
Their voices cold as winter,
Their wings grey as a cloud.
They've had nothing from my hands,
And I wish before dark fall
Some comfort for us all.

Skulls

Last night the snow came,
And again we face
Honest weather. The fence
That held its rose
So lightly is bent now
Under splintering snow.
It's winter. A flint cold
Has turned the house around

And the door hums in the wind.
If I went into the field,
Hearing the dry trees groan
In their barren cracking,
I would feel bones
Underfoot, winter's bones
Through snow, the furrow
Harder than the plough.

The ground's bone-hard. I first
Heard this in a place
Where snow was kindness.
Amazed, we had forced
Hard grass with our boots

Until it snapped. The clouds
Were scooped by easterlies
That set us hopping. It was

Our pink bones we imagined
Broken on that playground.
Long after a long snow,
After its memory,
When the sky had grown
Generously warm and sudden
Over as much world
As I remembered,

I went through a clarity
Of light in the early
Morning. And I climbed,
Climbed higher in the warmed
Hills than ever before.
Far away the sea
Burned, but I turned
To the last height

The growing sun could reach;
Then over it. Winter's touch
Lay there, unflawed
In a lake of snow
Below the peak. It was
A still depth, silence
For the raven's eye,
Holding its circled

Cold against the wreck
Of warmer seasons. Sprawled rock
Marked it, and a little
Moss. That world was all
Stillness; there was
No breathing in the place.
Skulls, the skulls of
Ponies, lay calmly dead above

The three-month snow, neckbones
Bent into snow, snow
Between the yellower hoops
Of their ribs. I had
Surprised them in their old
Deaths. Meek, vulnerable,
Stripped of flesh, muscle,
The last excuse of sinew,

They lay in a season
Too deep for sun,
For any weather to bother them.
Should the hornet
Perch in the empty
Pit of the eye, they
Would not startle. Let
Solid ice form

Its weight of the waterfall,
They would not huddle
Under the cliff. Their
Teeth, innocent of fear,
Were bare for birds to
Pick over. I let them lie,
The low dead in their cold
While I caught at the comfort

Of breath. When I let fly
A wild call through
The hilly dark, momently
The birds eased from the
Ledges, croaked, then
Lofted home. Again
I called, but nothing moved.
A mountain silence filled

The rock crevices.
I think of those open skulls
When winter comes, and coldest

Air reveals us. I lace
Heavy boots, break brittle ice,
Feel winter's bones
Under the snow. I hold
My skull to the wind.

Bridges

Imagine the bridge launched, its one foot
Clamped hard on bedrock, and such grace
In its growth it resembles flying, is flight
Almost. It is not chance when they speak
Of throwing a bridge; it leaves behind a track
Of its parallel rise and fall, solid
In quarried stone, in timber, in milled
Alloy under stress. A bridge is

The path of flight. A friend, a soldier,
Built a laughable wartime bridge over
Some unknown river. In featureless night
He threw from each slid bank the images
Of his crossing, working in whispers, under
Failing lamps. As they built, braced spars
Bolted taut the great steel plugs, he hoped
His bridge would stand in brawny daylight, complete,

The two halves miraculously knit. But
It didn't. Airily they floated above
Midstream, going nowhere, separate
Beginnings of different bridges, offering
The policies of inaction, neither coming
Nor going. His rough men cursed, sloped off,
Forded quite easily a mile lower.
It was shallow enough for his Land Rover.

I have a bridge over a stream. Four
Wooden sleepers, simple, direct. After rain,
Very slippery. I rarely cross right over,
Preferring to stand, watching the grain
On running water. I like such bridges best,
River bridges on which men always stand,
In quiet places. Unless I could have that other,
A bridge launched, hovering, wondering where to land.

The Twelve Stones of Pentre Ifan

The wind
Over my shoulder
Blows from the cold of time.

It has
Shaped the hill,
It has honed the rock outcrops

With the
Granules of its
Rasping. When the old ones

Were born
They dropped in dark-
ness, like sheep, and hot animals

Howled for
The afterbirths.
I watch the great stones of

Faith they
Moved in the flickering
Mountains of their nameless

Lives, and
See once more the
Points of adjusted rock, taller

Than any
Man who will ever
Stand where I stand, lifting their hope

In still,
Huge stone, pointed
To the flying wind. The sea ebbs again,

And round
The endless brevity
Of the seasons the old men's cromlech

Prepares
Its hard shallows.
The four great stones, elate and springing,

And the
Smaller stones, big
As a man, leaning in, supporting.

Elegy for David Beynon

David, we must have looked comic, sitting
there at next desks; your legs stretched
half-way down the classroom, while
my feet hung a free inch above

the floor. I remember, too, down
at The Gwynne's Field, at the side
of the little Taff, dancing with
laughing fury as you caught

effortlessly at the line-out, sliding
the ball over my head direct to
the outside-half. That was Cyril
Theophilus, who died in his quiet

so long ago that only I, perhaps,
remember he'd hold the ball one-handed
on his thin stomach as he turned
to run. Even there you were careful

to miss us with your scattering
knees as you bumped through
for yet another try. Buffeted
we were, but cheered too by our

unhurt presumption in believing
we could ever have pulled you down.
I think those children, those who died
under your arms in the crushed school,

would understand that I make this
your elegy. I know the face you had,
have walked with you enough mornings
under the fallen leaves. Theirs is

the great anonymous tragedy one word
will summarise. Aberfan, I write it
for them here, knowing we've paid to it
our shabby pence, and now it can be stored

with whatever names there are where
children end their briefest pilgrimage.
I cannot find the words for you, David. These
are too long, too many; and not enough.

A Small War

Climbing from Merthyr through the dew of August mornings
When I was a centaur-cyclist, on the skills of wheels
I'd loop past The Storey Arms, past steaming lorries
Stopped for flasks of early tea, and fall into Breconshire.
A thin road under black Fan Frynych — which keeps its winter
Shillings long through spring — took me to the Senni valley.

That was my plenty, to rest on the narrow saddle
Looking down on the farms, letting the simple noises
Come singly up. It was there I saw a ring-ousel
Wearing the white gash of his mountains; but every
Sparrow's feather in that valley was rare, golden,
Perfect. It was an Eden fourteen miles from home.

Evan Drew, my second cousin, lived there. A long, slow man
With a brown gaze I remember him. From a hill farm
Somewhere on the slope above Heol Senni he sent his sons,
Boys a little older than I, to the Second World War.
They rode their ponies to the station, they waved
Goodbye, they circled the spitting sky above Europe.

I would not fight for Wales, the great battle-cries
Do not arouse me. I keep short boundaries holy,
Those my eyes have recognised and my heart has known
As welcome. Nor would I fight for her language. I spend
My few pence of Welsh to amuse my friends, to comment
On the weather. They carry no thought that could be mine.

It's the small wars I understand. So now that forty
People lock their gates in Senni, keeping the water out
With frailest barriers of love and anger, I'd fight for them.
Five miles of land, enough small farms to make a heaven,
Are easily trapped on the drawing-board, a decision
Of the pen drowns all. Yes, the great towns need.

The humming water, yes, I have taken my rods to other
Swimming valleys and happily fished above the vanished
Fields. I know the arguments. It is a handful of earth
I will not argue with, and the slow cattle swinging weightily
Home. When I open the taps in my English bathroom
I am surprised they do not run with Breconshire blood.

Rhydcymerau

(after the Welsh of Gwenallt, 1899-1968)

The green blades are planted to be timber for the third war,
In the earth of Esgeir-ceir and the meadows of Tir-bach,
Near Rhydcymerau.

I remember my grandmother at Esgeir-ceir,
Pleating her apron by the fire,
The skin of her face as yellow as a manuscript of Peniarth,
And the old Welsh on her lips, the Welsh of Pantycelyn.
She was part of the Puritan Wales of the last century.
I never saw my grandfather, but he was a character,
A small, quick, dancing creature —
And fond of his pint.
He had bounced straight out of the eighteenth century.
They raised nine children;
Poets, deacons, Sunday School teachers,
The natural leaders of that small community.

My uncle Dafydd, nature poet and local wit
Used to farm Tir-bach.
His sly little song about the rooster was famous in the farms:
            'The little cockerel is scratching
            Now here, now there, about the garden.'
I spent my summer holidays with him,
Watching the sheep, and making lines of cynghanedd,

Englynion and eight-line songs in seven-eight measure.
He in turn had eight children,
The first a minister with the Calvanistic Methodists,
And also a poet.
We were a nest of poets in our family.

And now there are the trees, only the trees.
Usurping roots sucking the old soil dry;
Trees, where once it was neighbourly,
An army of forest where clean pasture was,
The bastard Saxon of the south instead of poetry and scripture.
The dry cough of the fox has precedence
Over the voices of child and lamb.

And in the dark centre
Is the lair
Of the English Minotaur;
And on the trees
As on crosses
The bones of poets, deacons, preachers and teachers of
     Sunday School
Bleach in the sun.
And the torrent of rain washes them, they are dried by the
     rubbing wind.

Wthan Moonfields

These are my fields in the moon's frost,
The summer coldness

Which is the night's alert while we keep abed;
And I am sleepless

Walking the dry, white meadows where,
A fortnight since,

Alun brought his scything tractor. Already
It is the newer grass

I bend with my thin slippers, already
The fragile pressures

Of my passing blacken under the moon, with
Finite shadows

Blacken. In the morning, temporary sun
Persuading us,

I'll walk warm abroad; but now I turn
Under the querulous

Owls for what comfort I can arrange
From darkness,

From summer ice. I know them well
The Wthan moonfields.

Water Voices

Christmas Day

Winter drought, and a parched wind
Roughens the mud. Wrapped in a parka,
Leaning bleakly into the slack
The blast misses as it screams over

The blackthorn, I'm tramping a
Chalk ditch from the downs. Leaves
Dry as cornflakes crack under
My gumboots, the hedge is against

My shoulder. Sands of their flying
Dusts hunt the spent fields, ice
Grains stick at my eyes. Caught
On the thorns, a rip of newsprint

Shivers its yellow edges, grows
Long, then rises easily, a narrow
Heron, out of shadow. It rises,
Trailing its thin legs, into cold

Sun flat as the land. Upright,
Broad wings spread, neck curved
And head and great blade turned
Down on the lit breast, it hangs

Against barbs, against winter
Darkness, before its slow vanes
Beat once over the elms, a
Christ crucified, a flying Christ.

Lear at Fifty

This morning early, driving the lanes in my
  Glib metal, frost fur on the brambles,
The grass, the hasps and bars of gates, first
  Sun burning it away in clinging wisps,
I saw an old man, sweeping leaves together, outside
  The Black Horse. His face held night's

Stupor, the lines of his age had not stiffened
  Against the daylight. He shifted his
Feet to careful standing, and then his broom,
  His necessary crutch, moved like an
Insect on slow, frail, crawling legs from
  Leaf to leaf. The small gusts of

My passing broke his labour, heaps of the dry
  Work spilling and flying. Nobody
Walked on the shore. Waves, unexpected heavy waves
  From some wild, piling storm away at sea,
Ripped the mild sand, smashed rocks, and shot the
  Squalling gulls out of the filth, vomit

And glittering sewage the flung birds flocked for.
  And truly, the tide was high this morning;
Old shoes, cans, cynical gouts of accidental oil,
  Plastic bottles, ropes, bubbling detergent
Slime, all were thrown to the sea wall. I have
  No wish to remember those unwelcoming

Waves I turned my back on, nor to think of old men
  Sitting tight in their skulls, aghast
At what their soft, insistent mouths will keep on
  Yelling. But through the limpet hours
I've walked the fields as if on a cliff's edge,
  The idea of flight in me, and seen my

Friends, myself, all strong, governing men, turned
    Sticks, turned tottering old fools.
The last sun in its blaze brings yellow light
    To everything, walls, windows, water;
A false warmth. In the morning some old man will start
    To sweep his leaves to a neatness.

i.m. James Chuang, MB, BS, MRCS, RN

(died April 23 1978, aged 25)

Last Thursday morning, watching a haul of barges
tug their blunt ropes under Chelsea Bridge,
I saw two swallows, hot from Africa,
flick and scream across the delighted river.
First of the warming year, emblem and omen,
one for each day of all that remained of your life.

Jim, I can't understand how anyone as young
and generous could go so swiftly into death.
It was good that afternoon, walking in Hyde Park,
watching the little goldeneye, pair by pair
in meticulous black and white, bobbing
on the cold Serpentine. To see them dive!

They'd slip under the water so casually,
without taking breath, without preparation
slide into the silence, longer and deeper,
until we couldn't see them. They all came back.
One by one all popped up from their underworld,
out of their darkness. Small London children,

playing with grandparents, clapped their hands
at each abrupt return. We spoke of your work
at Greenwich Hospital, the Seamen's Hospital
down by the widening Thames, and I was startled
by the wholeness of your compassion, your serious
tolerance. You were a chosen man. Somewhere

away from my awareness you had come of age.
And since then I've been finding it difficult
to remember you as a small boy, that brush-head,
the apricot-coloured child who would bring his
reading book, or that older one in Christ's
Hospital blue, alert, smiling, always eager.

On Thursday afternoon I knew you the full man,
conscious of healing, able to keep death at bay
down there near the river. Images of your childhood
were not wanted. You had become my contemporary,
although you were young enough to clap your hands
with the children, and I stand in an older body.

(Conscious of certain wreck, Jim, I had meant
to ask about arthritis, how my fingers stiffen;
but had not thought to know the pain of knocking
these words out.) To think a starling's nest,
untidy tangle of instinct pressed messily
into an air vent, could have killed you.

Anger meant little to you. If I am angry
it is a futility you must allow me now.
Two Canada geese, those heavy winter birds,
grey on a grey sky, beat overhead, trailing
silence behind their ponderous flying.
A cold evening has come back to the country.

Ponies

Stepping delicately, the ponies, the palominos,
Yellower than cream, smooth as butter, as bright
As the swags of ragwort they step among.

Stones in the river Brân, rounded as bubbles,
Limestone and sandstone tumbled from Fwng and Cedny,
And brilliant shallow water over them.

Heavy over the viaduct the belligerent engine,
Imminent, cloudless thunder beneath the arches,
A young man's tombstone under the hollow echo.

> *A white rose, his quiet life*
> *Fell in quiet to his grave.*
> *Quiet now, without a breeze,*
> *He sleeps in quiet, sleeps in peace.*

Unmoving, in an old darkness near the river,
The inquisitive ponies, the mild palominos,
Standing among hawthorns, snags of wild roses.

Lines for the Bastard Prince

His father's empty coffin, chipped
from the stone with a driven chisel
to keep the old man cold. Here spread
his hollow shoulders, and there

his ankle-bones were clipped. The air
and powder of those flying bones are lost.
But the boy's different. A blunt middle-weight,
balanced, powerful, such energy's even about

125

his rest his effigy can scarcely hold him in.
Oh, he was a tough one, neat and brutal
in attack, with a fast counter. His mother
was a fresh girl from the villages, her

blood could not expect the honour
of a cut tomb in the chapel, she did not
earn for her feet a carved dog, symbol
of fidelity. This firm prince is her memorial.

At the Sea's Edge, In Pembrokeshire

Peter de Leia, dead eight
hundred years, began this
structure. Not having the
saint's art, nor learned
his psalter from a gold-
beaked pigeon, he built
in common stone. He exalted
labour into a stone praise.

Nor was he baptised in live
waters conveniently burst
forth to supply the shaken
drops for that ceremony. To
reach his pulpit he climbed
a joiner's steps, did not expect
the ground to lift in a sudden
hillock so that he could preach
in open piety to the rapt Welsh.

When he laid down the square-
ended presbytery, with aisles,
transepts, tower and nave, he saw
his masons bleed if the chisel

slipped. One fell in his sight
from the brittle scaffolding
and the two legs snapped
audibly, hitting the ground.
He had not the saint's skill

to stop that falling which must
fall. Such clear faith was not
possible, the rule of the world
grown strong. He knew that right
building was a moral force, that
stone can grow. An earthquake
has tested this cathedral. In
Pembrokeshire, near the saint's
river, at the edge of the sea,

de Leia built well, saw stone
vault and flower. A plain man,
building in faith where God
had touched the saint, he saw
the miracle which is not swift
visitation, nor an incredible
suspension of the commonplace,
but the church grown great about us,
as if the first stone were a seed.

Once Upon A Time

(from the Norwegian of Tarjei Vesaas)

There was this little birch tree
And they said she should have leaves
By mid-May.
She could have danced, almost,
For that promise
And because she was as skinny as a child.

127

But first, they said, there would come
A warm wind; and he did.
He teased her, he waltzed her around, she was
Dizzy and sweet and tender
In every bud.
And when the bird came
And sat on a thin twig
Singing, Now, it's Now —

She didn't understand at all,
Not at all.
But in the evening
She stood slender and gowned
In her freshness, her translucent new green,
And she was absolutely transformed.

She turned about slowly,
Loosening herself quite free of dirt.
Ho hum, she sang, very quietly, now
To sail, like a green veil, over the hill,
For ever, away for ever
— Said the little birch tree.

Unchanging

Every seven years, is it, the body's
Changed? Flake by dry flake the skin
Renewed, glands and muscles altered
Secretly in their smooth liquids?
Hair, nails, how we shear them away,
Slow modifications unnoticed almost,
Until one day an accident of the mirror
Shows the remade man, grown different

128

Silently. All's changed then; eyes,
Manipulation of the senses, the very
Instruments of love are changed. The world's
Grown calcinous. What miracle, when
That which we call the heart is still
Immutable constancy, unchanged love.

Moonman

Last night I walked under the moon,
One of its green shadows, my eyes
A reflection of the chill moon.

Rounder than harvest, more cold
Than remembered frost, it burned
With sterile ardour the skin

Of the lane I walked. I know
It will be diminished, pared
Crescent recognisably, but say

It must grow again in its due time
More coldly blazing for the sleek
Ice to come. I had not thought

How I, too, wane as you turn away
Your sunlight, am great only
In harvests of your love.

Cave Paintings

i   After Dark

After dark, police sirens rip us
Awake. We crouch, hands over ears, our walls
Too small to hold such raucous invasion.

In Woodland Park, in caves
Of municipal concrete, the wolf
Shivers, the cougar shakes her chained ears.

ii   A Dish of Pebbles

Pebbles in a dish: opal, jade,
And one against sufficient light
A palpable smoke. All these

Are from Californian beaches. But here's
From Oregon a stone, from the castellated
Rim of the continent, its moats holding

Sea lions, voices of moist caves. Spray
Decorates the sky, the rattle of draining
Pebbles runs south from river-mouth to river-

Mouth. Here are sharks' teeth, two, for
Needling, bloodletting. And I have arrowheads:
This, from Washington; that, of greater age, from Somerset.

ii   A Thrush

The thrush comes into the house, I hear
Its soft battering against the window glass.

And I leave my desk, speaking to it,
Tolerate its panic, its round, wild eye,

The way it spreads its wings in a bare
Ache against the pane. I am accustomed.

To creatures, release it. It leaves behind
Two slight feathers, the yellow stain of its droppings.

iv Ancestor

There is no photograph, but I think him
Tall. He stood in twenty acres of grass
And a whole unfenced mountain uprose

Behind him. Certainly he worked
Eight sons timid, ruled all daylight,
Roaring at animals. Left, at the end,

Nothing, but was the last of us, long
Ago, to come off that brutal soil with
Innocent power. So I think him tall.

v In Still Clay

A Staffordshire greyhound, fawn, couchant,
Thin, stylised neck and flexible white hocks,
He sits in still clay on a dais of royal blue.

Six inches in length, the glaze crazed
Nowhere, and one gold line untarnished
Along the hollow plinth, he is preserved

By lucky accident. Pharoahs knew his like.
He dreams in the shadow between two shelves,
Linking time with time. Is a potent hunter.

vi   Scatterings of Light

Waterfalls, pools, streams, rivers,
And the loud, monotonous, empty

Drop through the centuries; the cave
Remembers water, was drilled

By water. Scatterings
Of light floated among bats

Pendulous as fruit in the rock's
Cold branches. A dry cave holds

Darkness to its walls, as water
Holds the shape of its flowing.

vii   Paperweight

This domed, heavy glass, it satisfies
The hand. Its concentric flowers, whorls,

Shells and coloured rods, its airy
Bubbles even, all are held in a still

Dance. I keep it for its solid
Roundness against time, and for the men,

In France two hundred years ago, who by
Some perfect means of their mortality

Made it, full and heavy, from fragile silicas,
And sent its casual permanence to my hand.

viii   Symbols

Emblems, plaques, icons, symbols
Of the decaying hand; stones, or

Feathers, identified by warm
Sight, and touched, and put

Aside; or voices,
Transferred as they vanish

In handled syllables, we keep
From the breaking dust, against

The filling of the cave. For
The cave is filling, fills

Rapidly. It closes,
From the eyes in.

Grooming

The poem stands on its firm
legs. Its claws are filed, brush
and curry-comb have worked
with the hissing groom to polish

its smooth pelt. All morning, hair
by hair, I've plucked away each small
excess; remains no trace of
barbering, and all feels natural.

It is conditioned to walk, turn
to the frailest leash, swing
without effort into ecstatic
hunting. Now I am cleaning

the teeth in its lion jaws
with an old brush. I'll set it
wild on the running street, aimed
at the hamstring, the soft throat.

Hyperion

was hardly a Titan. He stood
a brief inch over six feet, was
sweetly made. Not for his size
am I sent in his just praise
along the measured tracks

of his achievement. Dropped
on the printed turf by Selene,
daughter of Serenissima, he moved
even in his first uncertainty
like one waited for. His birth

was in green April, and he grew
in light, on the fat meadows.
Gently schooled, he delighted
his mentors with his perfect ardour,
honesty, the speed of his response.

Though small, he was quite beautiful,
his chestnut mane burning, his step
luminous. Some doubted his courage,
looking askance at the delicacy
of his white feet, ignoring the star

already brilliant in his forehead.
His heart was a vivid instrument
drumming for victory, loin and muscle
could stretch and flex in eating
leaps. When he ran, when he ran

the rings of his nostrils were scarlet,
the white foam spun away from his lips.
For his was the old, true blood,
untainted in his veins' walls:
two lines to St Simon, two lines

to Bend Or: The Flying Dutchman,
Bayardo, Galopin, all the great ones
back in his pedigree met in him.
He could not fail to honour
his fathers in the proud flood

of his winning. Nine times he left
his crescent grooves in the cheering
grass before the commoners gasped
after him. At Epsom, racing as if
alone on the classic track, he won

a record Derby, at Doncaster the Leger.
He won the Chester Vase, the Prince
of Wales's Stakes. Nor in his fullness,
drowsing in quiet fields in quiet company,
was he forgotten. His children,

sons and daughters of the Sun,
did not allow this. Hypericum,
Sun Chariot, Rising Light, all
were his. And Sun Stream, Midas,
Owen Tudor, Suncastle, many others.

The swift Godiva was his, and in
his image famous Citation, who ran
away with all America. Sportsmen,
all who go to the races, who marvel
at the flying hooves, remember Hyperion.

Ormonde

The great Ormonde was a roarer —
unsound in wind: but was never beaten.

The loud blemish of his flesh
suggests mortality, that he was

to be reached by some pretender.
It was a deceitful flaw. The horse

was perfect. Winning the Guineas,
'he took despotic command, sped

forward, galloped over everything,
won cantering'. So John Porter

of Kingsclere, his trainer, exulting.
Carrying unjust weight, he was ridden,

by Archer often, to extravagant wins
in great events, was led in his fame

over the Thames to Park Lane, where all,
at their champagne, were delighted

by his charm, his grave manners. He ate
his sugar from ladies' gloved fingers

and went amiably home. After which
the ingrate Duke of Westminster sold him;

sold to the Argentine his greatness, the
one Ormonde. His few offspring never

lived up to him. How could they,
measured against perfection, do other

than disappoint? Even in age, tendons
inflexible as bone, blunt clubs

too far from his thinning blood to sense
the turf, he would not be defeated.

I have to think that natural death
stood off in awe and would not take

the match on level terms. A bullet
killed him, smacking into his skull

before the old horse truly knew
he was under orders. As well he was

unprepared. He would have outrun death.

The beautiful young Devon Shorthorn Bull, Sexton Hyades 33rd

In warm meadows this bull
Ripens gently. He is a pod
Of milky seed, not ready yet.
Not liking to be alone, he
Drifts on neat feet to be near
His herd, is sad at gates
When one is taken from him. There's
No red in his eye, he does not
Know he's strong, but mildly

Pushes down hedges, can carry
A fence unnoticed on his broad
Skull. His flat back measures
The horizon. Get a ladder, look
Over him. Dream that, one by one,
The far fields fill with his children, his soft daughters.

Eagle and Hummingbird

Demure water, soft summer water,
Its rolling boulders dropped, its carried logs
Cast white as salt upon some resting beach,
I throw my spinners here, those small, beaked suns
Turning through steelheads, cut-throat, and the
Five-pound salmon come from the sea too young
Along the green channel of their instinct.

I stand midstream on rock, its roots in water,
Using the air to fly my singing line,
The burning spindle drifting through the river,
The river alders burning in the sun;
United elements, the one forgiving world
In whose veined heart I stand in a blue morning
Beneath the flash of hummingbirds, the smoulder

Of fishing eagles. Water and sun, fire
And reflected fire, the hundred suns
The river's mirror carries under the trees,
Buoyancy of the light birds, all's here,
All, all is here. And my thin line holds now
The lure of the hummingbird, its spinning
Breast, and the hooked voice of the eagle.

Ravenna Bridge

Thinking he walked on air, he
Thrust each step, stretched straight
His ankle. We saw him lift
On thinnest stone between him-
self and earth, and then dip on.

Such undulant progress! Stern
Herons walk like that; but he
Just rose again into his
Highest possible smiling air,
Stepped seriously by us,

And kept for all himself
The edges, even, of his happiness.
Passing, we caught the recognition
Of his transfiguring sweet
Smoke. And so he stepped, he

Skipped, the thin boy, on narrow
Ravenna Bridge, itself a height
Over pines and sycamores. He
Danced above their heads. If
He'd hopped the handrail, had

Swayed into flight, fallen
To stony death among wood-doves,
We should have watched him. I did
Not stand as I felt, hand
To mouth in a still gasp, but

Coldly and relaxed, and saw the boy
Perform his happy legs across
Ravenna Bridge and up the hill
To Fifty-Second. We walked home,
Thanking his god, and ours.

Marymere Falls

At the lip of the falls, small
Ferns totter in green air, tilt,
Lodge in a light pushed sideways,
As water, its level lost, pauses,

Grows heavy, and throws its slow
Roar outward, and down. Spray
Frets the marginal fall, imprisons
Sunlight in thin screens, climbs,

So frail its grains, against
All reasonable falling. But
Arc's full centre, its glistening
Plummet, profoundly falls, and falls

In booming pools, scatters,
Claps its steady diving over
Running stones, its words the poem's
Words: splash, rainbow, thunder.

A Reading in Seattle

Cold snow covers the summer
Mountains; they do not reject it.
Seas towed from Asia, immense
Pacific waters, invade the bays,
Roll heavy the long coast, turn
With a shake of the spray
And splinter the bleached
Lumber, sieve the lion-
Coloured sand. Inland, with
Lakes and the tamed
Salt of the Sound, is the lovely
City, safe in its washed air,
Holding its bridges calmly,
Its trees and tended grass,
The welcome of its wooden
Houses. At night, many
Lamps glitter cleanly, form
Stars in reflecting water

By skittering winds disturbed,
By small boats softly home
From fishing. The people sleep
In a ring of Japanese hills.
A hundred miles away a cone-
Shaped mountain measures the light.

Rivers, the rivers too.
Drop by plain drop they fall
From the cracking glaciers,
Collect in forming channels,
Roar, released, torrent of jade,
Opalescent fluid jewel,
Route of the salmon's instinct.
I stood once at the Skagit's edge
On a hot day, my face burned,
And walked slowly in, one step,
And another step, until I was
Waist deep in green flowing,
One with it, with the water.
Driving away through the little
Homesteads I was bereft. No man
Stands twice in the same river.

In the evening I thought
Of Dylan, how he had read
In Seattle. 'The little slob,'
My friend said, marvelling,
'He read Eliot so beautifully,
Jesus, I cried.' I did not answer.
In the city now the bars are
Empty of his stories
And only the downtown Indians
Are drunk as his memory.

I read in a hall full
Of friends, students, serious
Listeners. The great dead
Had spoken there, Auden,

Roethke, Watkins, many others.
There was room for a plump ghost.
I thought I heard his voice
Everywhere, after twenty years
Of famous death. The party over,
I walked home, saw on peaks
The coldest snow, white as bone.

Belonging

He came after the reading, when all
Had left, the students, the kind
Congratulating friends, and I was tired.

What it was gave me more than a
Public courtesy for this old man,
Small, neat in his blue suit, someone's

Grandfather, I can't say. He held
A paper faded as his eyes; his family
Tree. Anxious, erect, expecting my

Approval, he stood in the hot room.
'I'm Welsh,' he said. I read his
Pedigree. Bentley, Lawrence, Faulkner,

Graydon, no Welsh names. I nodded,
Gave back his folded pride, shook
My head in serious admiration. Belonging,

After all, is mostly matter of belief.
'I should have known you anywhere,' I said,
'For a Welshman.' He put away his chart,

Shook hands, walked into the foreign light.
I watched him go. Outside, the sprinklers,
Waving their spraying rainbows, kept America green.

Islands off Maine

(for Charles and Jeannie Wadsworth)

1

One man hammering
From his home on crevices
Shatters the darkness
Over the islands.

Dawn moves briskly
Among the rugosas
And the harbour lights take back
Their shaken images.

Water smooth as claws
Holds its silent traps;
On the visible tide
Floats huge America.

2

In the spring of the year eight ospreys
Flew over the island; smaller birds
Squalled at them, pollack and mackerel
Spun in their flustered shoals beneath

The seahawks' wings. Six flew on
To cull more northern waters; two stayed,

Perched much on trees, and hunted
Entirely in flight, circling. Hung

Two hundred feet above what fish
They chose; and fell, the vertical
Steep plunge between their own
Talons, then the consummate grab.

For surface fish they disturbed
No more than the sea's lace before
Flicking away water and taking off,
But can dive a yard into the packed

Ocean, feet braced thick against impact,
The toes lined with spicules, the claws
Stiff, and the whole battered water suddenly
Over their five-foot wings. They close

Their nostrils against the salt entry
And never fail. A sodden flap off
The surface they shiver away droplets,
Carry their fish head first, a torpedo.

All summer we saw their young in the
Flattened spruce top, all day we heard
Their mewling hunger, until they flew
On the cooling air, down the long coast.

3

And on the point one day,
Mist flattening the island,
I met the mad boy.

Brambles had torn his jeans,
His fingers were harsh as carrots,
Waterbeads dropped in his bull's curls.

His voice would not behave,
His skull was echoing and
The mist was behind his eyes.

'What d'you like about Maine,
Hey, what d'you like about it?'
Screaming like a blue jay.

Mountains, I told him, mostly
The mountains, but the sea too.
His joy was terrible, he hopped

In the gritty pebbles, he slapped
His laughing over the vague beach.
'Sure, there were mountains Monday

— today there ain't mountains!'
The island stopped where he pointed,
His hand wiped out Mount Cadillac.

'When you leaving, why don't you?
Why don't you leave? If you knew
The people here, you'd leave today!'

He moved away, was a stone, a
Post, a shape among shifting
Shapes, a slow uncertainty.

Unseen gulls jeered from the rocks.
Pewter light off the water
Faded when I hit the dirt path.

4

Pink Harding, born on the island,
Counts time in decades. Her chair
Rocks away anything smaller.

In all her years the sea has not stopped
Running. Each tide piles higher the granite
Pebbles, the red granite and the grey.

Hummingbirds visit her white phlox.
She is glad to hear this, but has seen
Them before. She is up since dawn.

We shout down her deafness, but scar tissue
Rubs at her eyes. She no longer braids
The tied rugs for which she's famous.

'Some I had ten dollars for!' she still
Marvels, 'And not always the best ones.'
They're heirlooms now, hang in museums.

She speaks of her father, that good man,
Then sits up, lifts one hand in pride,
'My grandfather was a full-blooded Englishman.'

5

Four white posts and a length of chain
Enclose the burial ground. Its stillness
Is twelve low headstones among the spruce.
You could walk past it, your head down

Against mosquitoes, and not see it.
Here lie the old, in the amplitude
And honour of their longevity: Capt.
Thos. Manchester, AE 92 yrs 3 mos;

Hannah, his Wife, AE 87 yrs 5 mos;
And nine others. But Gilman U. Stanley,
A boy, he sailed east and north
Out of Cranberry, past Novia Scotia,

In the temperate summer of 1861, watched
With his living eyes the Atlantic
Shake back the pack ice off Cape Breton.
All his life he'd seen harbour porpoise,

But now he called the finback whale,
The humpback whale, the minke and right
Whales as they rolled and mountained in their
Buoyant schools across the Cabot Strait.

Rich waters! O rich, destructive waters!
Working northward, never far from landfall,
They kept Anticosti to larboard, and Cape Whittle
And Little Mecatina Island; and saw on the right

The grave Newfoundland headlands where they
Should be, reaching on June 16 the Strait
Of Belle Isle. Where the boy at once went
Down. The sea took him, pressed flat

His agile breath, swam him among rocks
In water blue as ice, broke him in deep
Currents so that he lolled boneless.
Son of Jonathan R. and Irene Stanley,

AE 16 yrs 8 mos 28 dys. Each year the scrub,
The quiet moss, the little evergreens, move
Like a slow green tide on his empty grave,
Break on his headstone, and the other headstones.

6

water bell
    sea's angelus
        anchored edge of rock
and steep of water

toll for us

audible hanging wave
   simple element
      mouth of the round tide
storm's voice

      toll for us
   in our leaving

water tongue
   clapper and safe hammer
      sea's elegy and sound

   celebrate our passing

      toll for us

In Maine, September

Soon now, storm windows
Will shutter the island houses.
The hummingbirds are flown,
The summer people travel south
Towards their warming dollars.
Pretty little sailboats,
Bouncing on trolleys,
Move into sheltered winters.

Its silvered bleaching
Adrift on summer grasses
And a tide of dandelions,
An old boat lies in quiet
Behind the long point.
Is an exhausted animal,
Its lines the whale's lines,
For bludgeoning, for cutting water.

148

Travelling West

March ends, and the wild month
Batters its last hours against the house.
Such driven rain, such a wind
Bellowing out of the west
Against the walls!
I sit in the late room,
Watch the curtains shiver, and think
Of the drenched counties of England,
Their shuddering pastures, the creaking fibres
Of oak and hanging beech.

The gutters are full, the uneasy road's
Awash; dazed cars buffet the flood
Behind their swimming headlights.
Perhaps the grey sea from the west
Has broken in at last, bringing
Its ancient flotsam, news
From the drowned islands, voices,
Branches of legendary trees.
But that old, distant coast
Will hold, it will hold always.

Although I saw it when the year
Had barely turned from summer,
The sea was snarling early,
Spun me as I swam, thrashed me
Among its grains with its upper hand,
Sank me in little storms.
Fighting for land, gasping,
Reeling, beaten deaf, I saw
The small farms in the hills
Light up their steady lamps.

Flew west over a sea spotted
With cloud, and three days later
Swam in kindlier water,

In Branch Lake, by the Penobscot River.
Had gone for togue and landlocked salmon,
But the sun lulled my hooks. I hung
In a hammock of water, warm silt soft
To the toes. Mallard
Feathered above my comfort, the long
Westering light streamed through the red oaks.

I have walked hard Pacific beaches,
Skin burned raw by an insidious sun,
Stared through high arcs of spray
At seas running with tuna and oyster shell;
A man at the world's edge, facing westward,
Aware that every tide is for departures;
And came home, a small Odysseus,
Having, as best I could, followed the sun.
I sit alert in the still room, hearing
The storm, knowing no end to the journey.

The chalk downs hold these rains
Like a sponge, releasing them
Through the villages in clear bournes.
Salad cresses grow there, and tiny fish,
Their world a yard of shallow pool,
Flicker among the thready roots.
The flood will be absorbed and turned
To mild uses. Five hours will bring
The sun up. We'll begin once more,
Travelling west, travelling west!

New Poems, 1986

Berries

For the first time this year, berries
light up the garden. Stumbling downstairs,

grumbling, stubbing my sight against
a darkness I'm not ready for, I reach

for a switch, pause. In the garden
berries are incandescent. Frost

has uncovered the branches. Ignited fruit,
cotoneaster, holly, plump heps of damask,

of rosa rugosa, of the dry old noisette
nailed to the cold wall, all are blazing.

I stare in my dim awareness of autumn
passing, imagine how all over England

these sparks are lighting the winter;
round crab, the seeds of spindle

and wayfarer, clusters of buttery haw,
the waxy barberry, the black lamps

of ivy, beads of neglected briar,
of alder buckthorn, succulent

candles of yew. Perched on a chair,
I relish berries, warmed by their fatness.

Earth

Hail rattles the garden.
It scatters like white shot and
  The stung earth winces.

In summer I longed for
A cold wind. Now my neck aches
  At the first of winter.

Too late, too late!
The apple-blossom is blown and
  The sweet fruit gathered.

Like fish-scales the shine
On village roofs. The house prepares
  To reject winter.

As the leaves fall, so
The clouds multiply; it's all
  Balance, equilibrium.

Flints in the turned field,
The city's gutters, all things cry
  Endure, endure!

Dust in June, the field's
Stiff clay now; its puddles mirror
  The sullen weather.

When I was younger
I ignored dust; now I move near it,
  I watch it with love.

Is that the nestling
Which was featherless in May?
  He's hard-eyed now.

This morning the children
Raced to school. Who are these dotards
  Filling the schoolyard?

  'Consider this leaf,
Old now, dry as an egg-shell;
  It was born last April.'

  As I grow older
I begin to feel how strong
  The pull of gravity.

  Turning in heaven
The pied earth; its cities move
  Into daylight, darkness.

Six Poems from the Welsh
of Dafydd ap Gwilym

The Fox — Y Llwynog

Yesterday, while I waited
For my girl in the wildwood,
Confident she would come by
(In her time she's made me cry)
I saw in the trees' green gap
Not the heartbeat of my hope,
But the curse of our kennel,
A sly fox, red animal,
Sitting there on his haunches
As tame as a tortoise.

I aimed, since I had it by,
My new bow, yew and costly,
Intending with the use of arms
To set off a few alarms,
To aim from the hill's brow
A fast accurate arrow.
Too eager, I missed. Instead
Shot the wild shaft past his head;
And to make me more angry,
Broke my bow against a tree.

Then my fury at that fox,
That marauder of meek ducks,
That harrier of fat hens,
That glutton of goose-pens!
How he hates the horn's clear call
And the hounds on his trail!
His voice is not musical,
He glows against the gravel.
Ape-faced he flits the furrows,
Stalking a stupid goose,

Scaring crows at the hills's rim,
Acre-leaper, red as flame,
Observed by the birds' high eyes,
A dragon from old stories,
A tumult among feathers,
A red pelt, a torch of furs,
Traveller in earth's hollow,
Red glow at a closed window,
A copper box with quick tread,
Bloody pincers in his head.

Don't think to follow him where
Deep in Hell he has his lair.
Russet racer, scarlet dart,
He's too cunning to be caught.
Gorse-leaper, all graceful,
Leopard, lightning in his tail.

The Spear — Y Gwayw

I saw her there, her fair hair
Pale as foam, as white water,
From head to toe perfection,
More radiant than day-dawn.
She watched the play of Noah
In the saint's church at Bangor.
World's wonder and non pareil,
Pure flower and my betrayal,
Just to see her is for me
Greatest gift; and agony.

I'm stabbed with a seven-edged spear,
Each edge a complaint to her
That I lie pale with poison,
The gift of the men of Môn
Their envy is in my heart
And no man can pull it out.
No smith tempered this weapon,
No hand fine-ground its iron;
Without shape, without shadow,
A bitter barb brought its blow,
Subdued my splendour. I am ill
With love for Gwynedd's candle.
The long spear has pierced me,
My one thought is her beauty.
You may witness my weakness,
A sad boy with a white face,
Wearing her wounds in his heart,
Her painful skewer, her sharp dart.
She placed it there. I am killed
By a girl gold as Esyllt.

I'll wear her spear for an age,
Carry it in my rib's cage,
Endure the ache of the awl
Until death's dismissal.

The Seagull — Yr Wylan

Smooth gull on the sea's lagoon,
White as snow or the white moon,
Sun shard, gauntlet of the sea,
Untroubled is your beauty.
Buoyant you ride the rough tide,
A swift, proud, fish-eating bird.
Come to me, anchored on land,
Sea-lily, come to my hand.
White-robed, whiter than paper,
You're a sea-nun, sleek and pure.

Wide praise is for you and her;
Circle that castle tower,
Search till you see her, seagull,
Bright as Eigr on that wall.
Take all my pleading to her,
Tell her my life I offer.
Tell her, should she be alone —
Gently with that gentle one —
If she will not take me, I,
Losing her, must surely die.

I completely worship her.
Friends, no man ever loved more —
Taliesin's nor Merlin's eye
Saw a woman as lovely.
Copper-curled, curved as Venus,
How beautiful the girl is.
O seagull, but see her face,
Loveliest on the world's surface,
Then bring me her sweet greeting,
Or my certain death you bring.

The Girls of Llanbadarn —
Merched Llanbadarn

Plague take them, every female!
With longing I'm bent double,
Yet not one of them, not one,
Is kind to my condition.
Golden girl, wise wife, harsh witch,
All reject my patronage.

What's their mischief, what malice
Makes them turn on me like this?
That one, with the fine eyebrows,
Can't she meet me in the trees?
There's no blame, no shame on her
To greet me in my green lair.

I have always been someone
So prodigal of passion
Not a single day goes by
But one or two catch my eye;
But here they all think of me
As some kind of enemy.
Every Sunday in Llanbadarn
There I'd be (no need to warn)
Bemused by some girl's beauty
(But my back to God's bounty)
And when I had ogled all,
Sweet-faced in seat or stall,
I'd hear one of them whisper
To the wise friend beside her:

'See that pale boy over there,
With his sister's long hair —
Don't trust him. Look at his eyes,
They're sly and lascivious.'
'Is he like that? Then no chance,'
Says the friend, with a cold glance.

'He'll not get me, you may depend.
Let him roast till the world's end!'

What payment for my passion —
I've been sent to perdition.
I have to learn to restrain
My long pleasure in love's pain,
Must pack my bundles and flit,
A solitary hermit,
Must walk the world's cold boulder,
My head over my shoulder.
To look backwards, that's my fate,
A twisted neck, and no mate.

To Jesus Christ

Immortal Jesus, spirit — of God's spirit.
We know your pain was great;
Sharp stab of sword, then stretched straight
On the wooden cross, for man's merit.

Of your begetting the world knows — born
Of a virginal girl, God's called lass.
And at your birth, Lord, the clear stars — they sang
So early of you, *Dom'ne, Dom'nus,*
That three kings left their palaces — proud men
Travelling humbly to your low house,
Bringing their bountiful messages — bright gold
For You and your Mother, myrrh, frankincense.
True Father, Son of Grace — and Holy Spirit,
Shining Lord, the one Prince of our Peace,
Was it not arrogance — I ask sadly,
That sold our Trinity, our hope of miracles?
O treacherous Judas — O crude folly

To turn You to your enemies,
To animal torture, pitiless — brute blows,
   Your white limbs torn, thorns biting God's face.
And the voice of justice — a beggar-judge,
   A sycophant, pilate, son of beggars.
Now come the naked flatterers — thieves,
   The sweet deceivers, a throng of Jews.
Now nine step out with ropes — brought to bind you,
   For your sacred sake, to the pine cross.
So cruel the cut of cords, the knots — now Mary
   Cries a great call above her falling tears.
Even so the end was gracious — despite the Cross
   The cold grave could not keep you, Matthew says.
When we see it for ourselves — blest Passion,
   Why is it we don't think of your groans?
Your nailed feet fill (sad memories) — with blood,
   Aching for me, O God, your pierced hands;
On your beautiful head, the marks — of death,
   Your lips turn pale, your wounds leak from spears.
And for these sad injuries — God's ordeal,
   A hundred should attest your holiness.
From your harsh miseries — were we not blest,
   Suffering God, when you came to us?
After your death, for us — there is no evil;
   For Joseph too your life was welcome, Jesus.

Verses for the Mass — Englynion yr Offeren

Anima Christi, sanctifica me.
    Merciful, famous heart of Three — and One,
       The prophets' whole glory,
      Sweet soul of Christ from the tree,
      Polish me like a jewel, cleanse me.

Corpus Christi, salva me.
 Christ's stricken body, battered — without cause
  Communion's found bread,
  Find me not among the dead,
  With your life keep mine protected.

Sanguis Christi, inebria me.
 Christ's blood, lest for wildness — I am sent
  Into the wilderness,
  Then rise, light of God's praise,
  And keep me from drunkenness.

Aqua lateris, Christi, lava me.
 Waters of Christ's wide scars — His sore side,
  Bravely he bore the Cross —
  In those eternal waters
  Let me wash, count me no loss.

Passio Christi, comforta me.
 Christ, heaven's passion, leader — lord of prophets,
  Your five wounds were bitter;
  But strong is the power of prayer,
  Strengthen me, uphold me, Sir.

O bone Iesu, exaudi me.
 Compassionate Jesus, turn to me — a speck;
  Turn, Light of the new day;
  Lord of all worship, hear me,
  Listen, do not condemn me.

Et ne permittas me separari a te.
 Place me, my whole self, my soul — rich increase,
  Near your hand, world's weal;
  Like a strong hedge, I'll serve well,
  Praise without pause my voice tell.

Ut cum angelis tuis laudem te.

> With a holy throng, Lord, your strong host — angels,
>> Light that will not be lost,
>> You call from heaven's high post
>> That we shall be saved and blest.

Amen.

> Let us come to that true kingdom — heaven,
>> In obedience come;
>> Land of high grace, eternal welcome,
>> Land of our faith's feasting, home.

A Sea in the Desert

The Hawk's Eye

(for Fred Ewoldt)

The hawk carries his eye
out of swinging altitudes
higher than winter.
Above his locked feet,
hunched in wet feathers,
he rages in larches.
It is the snow brings him down.

Bland snow has covered
the rock of the precipice.
Is the hawk to hang
above so changed a world?
He knows the quiet architecture
of high places, the black
argument of granite.

But the snow's in his eye
and he shrieks in temper.
I could use that harsh gaze
above the crested summit
of fluted snow, and the curved
stretches of ledges.
I could look down

between the grasp of my arms
on the still air
and see in the dark
the stars of dark farms
in the huddle of winter,
their byres shut to the night
and their eyes turned to the fire.

I could see the men
I might have become
turn out of their stiff clothes
to sleep the cold night, fatigued,
under heavy blankets
woven by their mothers.
I could see a man,

perturbed, hearing foxes bark,
move with his lantern
across the muffled yard
into his barn
where the spent chaff,
light, lighter than air,
will rise in his little flame,

climb in the small heat,
motes, thin dust of old harvests,
until the man turns,
grumbling at the cold,
thumbs shut his latch
against the high snow
where the hawk is at watch.

These Hills, These Woods

Who comes out of these hills, these woods,
from the small white house in the hollow,
from the summer river between ferns?
Who travels the rough lanes worn

by the stumbling dung-cart? They carry
among the bundled clutter of clothes and pans
and the rattle of what is portable
the whole of their lives. That one,

larky, long in the leg, red-bearded, he
will not come back. Already his grave
is marked, he will not see his grandchildren.
The young one, who knows the flight

of lark and pipit and holds their bald nestlings
within his hands, will fall apprentice
to a butcher. He will run screaming
from the slaughterhouse, his eyes full

of hacked red meat, the round cries
of animals will follow him all his roads.
He will walk through the dark lots,
through brutal labour in furnaces,

through human betrayal. His sisters
will curb their thin tongues, laugh
bitterly and in secret; endure. They will
never return. It is I who recall their ghosts

to the house under the hill, their
wavering dust so frail it does not stir
the powder of the roads. It is I
who people the lanes of homecoming

and build the fallen chimneys stone by stone
so the doused fires will carry the echoes
of old warmth, and the fields hear more
than the hawk's voice, and the silence after.

Hawk Music

At this height I have to say
there are no boundaries
but those of river and bluff.

This eye ignores
the political world,
is concerned with what's visible.

Its happiness is to watch
the intricate valleys weathering
and the wearing down

of upturned faces of rock.
Let me lean into this wind,
so rare that its demands

are those of music. I would
give it a note on the thinnest
string of air, a sound

so high the ear cannot
support it. But I
will hope to hear it.

The Summer Hawk

I wait in blue light, for
early thermals, a hint
of lift. My arms stretch

in effortless recognition, in
widening order at the day's turn.
Counties are opening under me,

in daylight, for my regard;
their fields, sleeping houses
beneath their tiles. The sun's

on my back, the cross of my shadow
closes a wood of singers.
One tractor hangs the pale

of its exhaust against a hedge.
I begin to organize my patterns,
shadows that lean into darkness,

anglers tied to their water all down
the river. And in the meadows
cruel children hunt among flowers.

A Dying Hawk

She stoops and drops
through a straight
funnel of sight
into falling air.
She folds gravity
to her heart, and dives

behind her eye.
The one purpose
of her gaze
will not let her see
the clear windscreen
moving to kill her.

She spreads too late.
Her wings, her talons
set against air.
She dies at the roadside,
her hollow bones
are splintered

in the rags of her feathers,
and her brittle gape
is open and broken.
Before her head falls
what is left
stares from her yellow eye.

The Hawk Maps His Country

The river crawls to the sea.
I bring them down
through gullies of rain,
flatten them in valleys
slide their silver estuaries
into darker water.
Gulls ride the ripples,
svelte waterbirds, breathers
of a thicker air. Kittiwakes,
snickering herring gulls,
and in the reeds, white,
white as a pearl,
a single ivory gull,
eater of excrement.

A populace of shorebirds
struts the yellow ledge
between land and water.
Stilts, knots, sharp snipe,
phalaropes in their variety,
avocets and sandpipers,
let them wade and preen,
petty turnstones,
community birds.

Flocks of goldeneyes
occupy the water,
mergansers, eiders,
a flight of cinnamon teal,
stiff-tailed, red.
Let them glow
in their common element,
and on domestic ponds
let Aylesburys paddle.

In a change of weather
the wild geese
fly their wide arrows
over my ranges,
yelping at night
as they pass under the moon,
a compass in their skulls.
I will not stop their lanes.
The seasons follow them.
They draw the sun behind them
birds of the tender meadows,
oiled against moisture.

My eye measures
the edges of the world.
I am centre and rim
of its only soaring.
I hold the high Sierras
in the grip of my claws.
I call, and it is my voice
answers. When at last
I tumble headlong
out of serene wheeling
I shall leave a cry
hanging beyond echo
in the sustenance of air.
The earth will be heavy
with the puff of my dust.

Hudson's Geese

'. . . I have, from time to time, related some incident of my boyhood, and these are contained in various chapters in *The Naturalist in La Plata, Birds and Man, Adventures Among Birds*. . . .'

W.H. Hudson, in *Far Away and Long Ago*.

Hudson tells us of them,
the two migrating geese,
she hurt in the wing
indomitably walking
the length of a continent,
and he wheeling above,
calling his distress.
They could not have lived.
Already I see her wing
scraped past the bone
as she drags it through rubble.
A fox, maybe, took her
in his snap jaws. And what
would he do, the point
of his circling gone?
The wilderness of his cry
falling through an air
turned instantly to winter
would warn the guns of him.
If a fowler dropped him,
let it have been quick,
pellets hitting brain
and heart so his weight
came down senseless,
and nothing but his body
to enter the dog's mouth.

The Hawk Climbs

The hawk climbs, and climbing,
seems to hang for ever;

but he too passes over the hill.
Once I found a hawk's skull,

dry, stern hook and bone,
not changed for centuries,

perfected. Yet the seasons
took him, for all his mastery.

I look through the hawk's lens
for an essence I guess at,

the place where his circling ends
and nothing turns into the dark.

Mice under the leaves, speckled
pebbles, I can see them; and

the small dust kicked up
by boys running from school.

I can feel hard growing
in the bones of such children.

There's not a movement
in the country of my eyes

which is not counted. But where
are the lean young men who live

for ever? How far are the fields
where broken ponies run, their legs

made whole? Where is that green
country which put an end to time?

Until that land is found
I search with the hawk's eye.

Islands

(for Garold Davis)

Summer's first day, earlier
if the sun were hot enough,
someone would think of water.
We'd run to search in cupboards
for our old swimming trunks,
roll them in towels,
and make our way upriver.
We'd pass the thinning houses
at the edge of town,
pass Pulman's cautious house
behind its wall, his raging
mastiff choking in its snarls.
Two fifty-six pound weights
dragged after him, slowed him.
Old Pulman came out sometimes,
shouting his nervous threats,
easing his beast to calm,
wiping the white froth
with his hands
from the dog's jowls.

But we would be long gone,
aimed for a green elbow
of the river, below the bridge,
where quiet water lingered.

In April once, early sun
deceiving us, we found
three taller boys
already in our pool,
hooting with brisk chill,
calling us to join them.
They could all swim,
floated downstream,
churned water, struck out
across the current.
But the tireless river
throughout its seasons
had filed a narrow channel,
deep, carrying hidden water.
It kept us splashing near the bank,
timid on shallow pebbles.

Boysie Wilde carried me across,
my small weight almost sinking him.
But he swam on, head lifted,
gasping, keeping his breath dry.
He set me in another country,
on the far side of danger,
waist deep in a strange river.
Little waves floated me,
bumped me inch by inch
down a stone ledge. I watched
my legs hang pale
in deep water. Later,
grown cold, I pushed away,
thrashed with my arms
above imagined fathoms,
crawled safely out. The kind
of useless daring I was good at.

That was the day Reg Smith,
knowing that Channel swimmers
cover themselves in grease
to still the cold,

brought half a pound of lard
to keep his white skin warm.
And in he stepped, laid his plumpness
in the clean river. At once
the fat slid off, spreading
in frailest rainbows, fled
in films until the broken shallows
took them.

Walking home, glowing,
we were fulfilled.

It was a known world then.
We lived in it, we made it
with our voices. Somewhere,
we had no doubt of it,
there would be islands
in which the temperate sun
allowed for daylong swimming.
In a world like ours
perfect things were probable.

Meanwhile we walked a world
sound to its very core.
Who could have thought
its crust so thin that men
would burn it dry, shatter it?

We did not imagine
our days were counted.

In Africa, Reg Smith, only child
of old parents, his body
wrapped in khaki, burned away
and vanished in his smoke.
With many others, appalled,
confused, all certainty gone.
They did not find the islands.

I have not found the islands,
islands of peace, of the blest;
but would believe in them,
would search for them, would
keep them floating,
with my breath.

At the Grave of Dylan Thomas

If I were young I could
Make eager grief of this grave
And let the warm sorrow come
And cover me like a wave,
The cathartic tears ease out
That soothe the constricted heart.

It would be over and done —
A romantic memory made
Out of this drift of rain
And the passive part I played.
Spontaneous youth is gone;
The moved heart is a stone.

Time makes a flint of the heart
That grief cannot spark into flame,
A stubborn, intractable weight
Moved but to inadequate blame.
Here, between hill and sea,
Resignation rules finally.

So I'll not denounce this death
Nor embitter the ordinary air
With blown words that my breath
Is now too small to wear.
Sufficient that he is gone;
A great man dies alone.

Headland, river and bay
Wait for the implied night,
And I, as I move away,
Accept a mutinous fate,
Accept the perpetual sea's
Recurrent elegies.

Seabirds adorning the hill
Move with a bickering grace
As each descending bird
Settles into its place.
Smoothly the plain day ends.
Nothing can make amends.

Christmas in Utah

In barns turned from the wind
the quarter-horses
twitch their laundered blankets.
Three Steller's Jays,
crests sharp as ice,
bejewel the pine tree.
Rough cold out of Idaho
bundles irrational tumbleweed
the length of Main Street.

Higher than snowpeaks,
shriller than the frost,
a brazen angel blows his silent trumpet.

The Dark Months

Frost nails to the soil
the slots of deer.
Snow will cover them
the dark months of the year.

Waxwings strip from the branch
last fleshes of berry —
haw and firethorn nourish
their starving journey.

It is an eternal star
above the high Uintas
offers its untouched light,
its cold promises.

A Message for Dafydd ap Gwilym

They tell me you were an aristocrat, Dafydd.
There were none in Merthyr Tydfil,

But for the upstart ghosts of the Crawshays
And old Doctor Ward from Victoria Street.

His was the comer house (with orchard)
Whose tumbled masonry lies in the dirty car park.

It took his housemaid three hours to polish
The great brass headlamps of his open tourer,
A Sunbeam, painted white, already vintage,
But very deeply loved, you could see that.

In steep, appalling rain he hoodless drove
From Dowlais Top, the fine stuff of his suit
Turned black with rain, his monocle awash,

The corrugations of his grimace draining water
Off that wild skull. From Rossi's doorway
I saluted him, without irony, intoning loud:

The chair he sat in, like a burnished throne.

Where there's no sense there's no feeling,
Said Tommy Probert, my fruity companion.

But I thought it patrician enough —
In the hour of its need he did not desert his car.
You might have agreed with Tommy Probert.

And once at a luncheon
I sat next to Lord Goodman.

In Cyfarthfa Castle School, reading around the class,
My turn was 'The Solitary Reaper'.
I read it well enough to make the teacher peevish.
You've learned that by heart, he grieved,
To spout at some eisteddfod. I agreed.
I had not seen it before, ever.

It's the words, of course, we can't leave them.
These for your ears, from the town's edge:
Pwllywhiaid, Castell Morlais, Caemaridwn.
And these, among the streets, for mine:
Incline Top, The Ballcourt, the Tramroad.

I've written, too, of those
Manifestations of the natural world,
Birchtrees, birdsong, the inconvenient
Snow, so often your concern.
Like you, I am from the south, like you
I had (in youth) the pale hair
You boast of; in youth
I was slender and thin-faced.

For these dubious affinities, Dafydd,
I tell you — though you have no need to ask —
Dafydd, you are not dead, you will not die.

Stones Trees Water

1

Sticks and stones
are what the tides let fall in haphazard
order; rubbed pebbles nesting in sand,
casual spars and twigs dark with continual
water, lolling in companies. And what
the rivers cast at summer's dry edges,
mark of the burly flood, measure
of the winter course, bleached now,
and quiet. And quiet the slow grating
of the rolling surface, helpless the soft twigs.
Impervious small round fragments
of mountain, splinters of soaked forest.

2

Walking the round limestone hills, above
the line where the chill springs bubble
from the stone clefts, we are aware
of the scarce trees. An elm, and
an elm, and at the edge of our sight
three more in a still dance. And no more,
however we may look. Why is it, after
a day's walking on this sweet grass, we see
the rooted trees still with us, an elm,
an elm, and three quiet elms far off,
poised for dancing?

3

Impossible to see the first pale
tendrils, thinner than hair, frail,
diffident, inexorably working the long
seasons for a true grasp of earth.
And ripening in time so that the grown tree,
its whole upright leafing,
is held by the roots' great fist
clamped about rock and cavity,
sleek shoots thickened and hardened.
We do not see the tenuous, early
pluck at the thin skin of the world,
but look now at the admirable
driving power of the rooted beech!

4

What trick of the strengthening
light, what angle of the tilting world
to the sun, what is the alarm
that sets the trees to work?
Solitary in grazed meadows,
or grouped in copse and hanger, trees
ripen their plump buds
at some green signal
of returning spring.

5

The tree is a slow fountain, erupting
inch by inch
from a deep source
it creates for itself.
Balked, it pauses,
gathers its power
to lift away whatever prison

had thought to hold it down;
then moves purely upward, thrown slowly.
The tree spreads wide its elements,
they branch and fall,
subject to gravity;
a spray, a frail drift,
a falling away.

6

A great tree stands in its wide
shade; generous, still trunk.
Its branches, stalks, leaves
hold air and light. I stand
at its broad foot and think
of the rooted strength,
large as a tree, and branched,
wrapped about earth and stone,
grasping the spinning world.

7

Smooth bole of the beech tree, grey
as elephants, but not wrinkled,
it hides with tidy scars the snags
of dropped branches, and holds
to the light its scatterings
of pointed tawny buds and fresh green leaves.
In Slindon Woods, in a cathedral
of high beeches, the perfect one,
standing without shake or bend,
is called 'Beauty'. Someone,
with neat respect, has carved her name
on the mellow bark; and she, indifferent
to the name, has nearly healed it away.

8

In the beech wood, when light
is perfect green, underwater colour,
green of sunlight filtered
through prodigal green leaves, our hands
and upturned paler faces green, our
very walking and talking freshened
by green light —
then,
one branch of one tree, from its smallest
twig inward, changes; and all along
its length is radiant gold. So that we see
more clearly the green.

9

Grown tall, the trees stand
near my door, knock
on my wall. I need them
less for their globed fruit,
generous victoria, russet,
the streaky pippin, than for
the interweaving of their branches,
dark on a dark sky. I watch
their branched involvements
with the wind, and when, too dark
to see, I pull the blind across
their restlessness, my arms
reach upward, fingers
stretch like twigs.

10

Wealth of the beech, its spendthrift
copper pence are thrown in heaps
and drifts on sparse grass. Chaffinches

pick there, neat in their close feathers,
looking for beech nuts. Eddies and currents
of loose gusts blow the leaves. Dry,
tenacious, carried by water, wrecked
on roads and pavements, they do not rot,
are bountiful still in drifts and heaps,
and brave as single medals on the ground.
They see their green heirs swing above them.

11

Green winter sun touches the yearning poplars.
They stretch to it, creak their swaying trunks
in the brisk wind. Do they feel in their bent
terminal branches the stirring of the seasons?
Are the constrictions of the iron ground
painful to them? Momentary clouds
pass over them, their shadows scud
away. And high in the sudden, luminous
blue of the revealed sky, see there, the pale
enigmatic symbol of the daylight moon.

12

There are no simple seasons, sufficient
to themselves. Summer leaves,
swinging in glossy plenty from the boughs,
remind us of the January trees,
black in the cold rain. We tread
the old leaves underfoot,
leaves six months dead. We walk
among the brief generations of leaves
towards winter.

13

Revealed by winter, small trees
stand like rueful old men,
their bare shanks thin, their
old veins hardening. Useless
to promise as we walk among them
a renewal of youth, a returned
flaunting of green,
when April comes.
They are turned now
from the wind
that shaped their growing
and it is enough
that they endure
what each day's weather
brings to them.
And who is so rash
as to promise us
another April?

14

In a bitter night, if the mists
demand, trees are encased
in white dampness, trunk, branch
and twig; and solidifying frost
turns all such trees to glass.
I have seen an orchard of glass,
white as dawn, where I thought
to have found only solid Bramleys.
A whole country can be suspended
in deluding fog. Men, coming out
to their steaming flocks, will hear
trees crack and splinter, fibres
shredding beneath the tiny axe of ice.

15

As it falls, the tree squeals
in its fibres. Heavy, pulling apart
its dry strings, it bounces
once against the earth, and settles.
Chainsaws slice it in coarse
roundels. What is left, brushwood,
torso, splintered ends
of branches, burns for days
in a corner of the field. Smoke
drifts under the hedge. Darkness
uncovers small red stars
flaring in the soft ash.

16

Winter strips the wood. Bones
of snapped bramble litter the hedges.
Pale moths, frail as paper, fall
in the moon from cracks of bark.
I walk in the cold light, hearing
the trees complain from their stiffened branches,
seeing grains of frost stiffen the yellow grass.

17

The stacked logs wait to blaze
to a quick ash their long, bright summers.
Lithe boughs that held the air
in a mesh of leaves, and swung
to the caprice of the free breeze,
are lopped blunt piles now,
for all their annual circles.
Fallen to saws and chopped
in fireside lengths, they dry away
their old sweet Aprils, and shrink
from their harsh, dry bark.

18

Under the hill a shadow
hides all in its small night, tree,
stone, grass cropped short by rabbits.
And it moves to cover, as earth
turns over into darkness, the black
tree, black grass, sleeping fields
turned up to night. Night's breath
is soft as shadows under the hill.

19

Monotonous winds
invade the fields, the empty spaces.
Bleak light reveals the trees,
blunt stumps of trunks, cracked
branches, rubbed, cancerous bark;
old scars of surviving.
We walk the broken wood
as through another war. Winter
rehearses the end of the world.

20

The winter water wears its pure skin,
ablaze with cold light. Tottering
flocks of mallard, their webs
bemused, search for their floating
element; but the water's hard,
is glass and mirror. On banks the bents
and tussocks, tipped with frost,
turn lank and pale. The ice burns
with clear fire, by day by night.

21

To live with water. To walk over
water meadows, to know the seasons
of change and renewal in the colonies
of water, in the proliferation
of water-crowfoot, the flowering
and seeding of yellow flags; to judge
the heat of summer evenings by the ease
of cattle knee-deep in country
water; to know winter by the stripped
canes of the willow, by the heron's
desperate stillness, the surprise
of ice. To live with water.

22

Boneless reeds betray the stream's
direction. Faults in the quick run,
stones, obstacles, vexing shallows,
all hold back the sticks' tangles, a float
of thick scum. Bright water
hurries under them.

23

Fire, the acid exhalation
of industrial chimneys, serpentine
breeding of highways: the trees
are dead. Where once the natural winter
took the weak, the shallow-rooted,
charred scars mark the paper skin
of the birch tree. The oak is dry.
Their heartwood is soft with fungus.

24

Rampart and wide ditch,
moat and stone keep
lie under the fists
of green bracken.

Barriers of enormous concrete,
long galleries safe from invasion,
all the complexities of defence
are lost to silent moss.

Rust covers the dry guns.

25

Under grass the living rock, sandstone,
or limestone; from earth's making.
However skilled the harsh drill
and set explosions of the quarry,
stone makes its protest, breaking
in unexpected seams of growth,
flaking. Handled in square blocks, ordered
by plumbline and level, it retains
its nature, its silence. It remembers
the seas which made it.

26

Something happens to a dry wall: the earth
has to accept it. It must be built
with due reverence for the curves and usages
of the land. A field has its own passages,
its underground, differing textures, can direct
the root of trees beneath a wall, point
small creatures into crevices, measuring,
reporting. And if a wall is made wrongly,

arrogantly cuts across the field's
own passages and ways, then a slow,
uplifting, irresistible heave, lasting
many seasons, compounded of cracking frost
and warmth and all growing things, undoes
the wall, breaks its dry bonds, topples it.
Don't think to repair it. Look humbly
at the land, build where the wall belongs.
A field knows its own boundaries.

27

Working with stone, now. There's something
in that. The slow modification
of shape, the chipped squareness of stone
as it takes shape against the blunt hammer,
the chisel. Then fitting the dressed stones
together, moving them those heavy fractions
so they fit, lock well, are solid in the wall.
And then to walk away, tired, knowing
what will happen. That the low stone wall
will weather amicably, accept fern
and lichen, settle into place
as if it grew there. Be a memorial
for all the anonymous men who work with stone.

28

Time wears on the flat cliff
its simple messages, cleans them
with rain, with the lunar orderliness
of the sea. Lichen and sopping moss,
those old communities, their growth
too small to measure, their surfaces
velvet on harsh stone, inhabit
the faint declivities. The manner

of the cliff is angular, its lines
clean and direct. It breaks
with a sharp, clear statement.

29

In slum pools at the edge of town,
in stinking hollows where garbage drains
its slimes of drums and rust,
among brittle, lifeless coils
and abandoned car seats,
the dead twigs lie. A film of stones
reflects a faint light.

30

Tight on the gull's bone
this feather held air
in the webs of its rays
and floated the tides
of turning winds.

But ripped from the bird
in its falling death
in the wind of the storm
it winnowed through air
to the still pool.

31

Where shall we rest?
cry stones, whose fate
is to knock about the world,
growing smaller, to fly
from slings and kill giants
while meaning no harm,

to mark boundaries and mileages,
to honour the dead
above their stale bones,
to be silent.

32

Gurgling and chortling
the smack of the tide
about the round
bluff of the cliff
sidles away
with a tumble
of little pebbles
and a wet buss
on the curves
of firm stone.
The plump limbs
of laved bluestone
wait for the work
of the turning moon.

33

Only bones are left
after the tongues of water
have lapped away what was loose
and friable; great bones
of the land and thin stone
fine as shoulder blades. Water
wears at the long orifices
of stone, grinds honeycombs
of entrances into the hard body
of rock, will return, will return.

34

Seawrack and stones in still pools
the sea leaves after it. Fronds
of lax weed the children love
to drag in leathery chains along
the sand, the bones of the skeletal
world when it was made, they
join here in casual pattern we search
for meaning, for significant omens.
But a wind ruffles the water's face.

35

Our scum floats at the edge
of water, a brown froth, drying
on stones. Where a river
falls over weirs, the waste
filth bobs on the tight
waves and sails, a raft
of bubbles, on gasping
water. There's a fascination
in watching our spoilage
float away, as if, for once,
we had become perfectly innocent,
as if the sea had carried away our dirt.
It is a delusion. Our scum
floats at the edge of the water, clings
to the stones on the shore.

36

Peninsulas, islands, stretches
and stands of rock,
firm on the seabed.
Out in the bay, an archipelago
of diminishing rocks, unmoving.

It is the water shifts
past such anchored settlements.

37

The conversation of stones is serene
and calm, has polished surfaces
and few empty silences, is concerned
often with weather
and with formal elements.
Stones do not yield, but will
lean harmoniously, one
to the other; are sociable
and fond of company.
Left alone, they are content to meditate,
usually on the possession of solid virtues.

38

On the beach, on ribbed sand
ridged by vanished tides,
among the courses of water
and raised edges of clams,
the boulders lift their animal
heads, and wait. Their gouged
sockets are soft with moss, their hides
scoured by rubbing grit.
Unmoved by the rise
and fall of the sea,
their breathing
is still as marble.

39

The sea carries above it
an enormous sky.
A path, dropping
through bracken and heather,
avoids rocks and running
water, scuttles beneath
dark heights on either side,
turns once upon itself,
and breaks through into the light.
The sea comes up to meet it.

40

Sea-fires cracked Shelley's bones.
He lay on the Pisan shore
and clean flames ate him.
There are worse ends
than suffocating waves of the sea,
a pyre of round stones,
green fires of driftwood.
On the beach, as the year dies,
I light this celebratory fire,
watch the blue smoke, rising.

41

I stand at the land's edge, waiting
for what the tide will bring to me
and what it will take away.

A Sea in the Desert

1

A little sea
    in the night
     ran its inch of tide
about the bole of the peach tree,

hesitated,
    came fawning to my door,
      cringed,
        fell away.

Its small crests,
    its ebb,
      broke my sleep.

2

A little sea
    was running in the desert.
  It came in
    under the edges of the breeze,
a true sea,
      sharpening the air with salt,
        filling hourly through the night.

It remembered white ships,
    clippers out of China
      freighted with tea and roses,
        sea-swans
    holding gales in their wings,
storms off the coast of fragrant Spain, snarling.

It hurled
against my walls
its gathering whips and drums,
dropped away,
its throat rattling with pebbles.

3

I got up,
opened my door
to this unbelievable sea.

My yard was lit by silent moonlight.
Parched grasshoppers chirrupped in the ditches.

4

But still the sea broke
on the beaches of my ears.

My skull was a shell
holding the noisy tides
Pouring unseen over the desert.

5

A man is moon to his own sea —
he draws it after him,
like a dog it follows him
the days of his life.

All that night I heard the sea make
and ebb, a sea formed
of grains of remembered oceans,
fed by rains and rivers

of days I had finished with.
It carried old sticks in its mouth.
In the morning a tide's detritus,
twigs, small round stones, a can,

lay in uneven lines
on the charred grass.

6

A hermit thrush sings for me
in dry arroyos its liquid note.
I have heard in the desert
unrecognised birds, charmers,

lift up their single whistles,
long separated, distant,
purified by distance, among
the grassless dunes.

I have thought them calling me.
I have heard the voices
of an invisible sea
whispering with boys'

voices, heard in its dry waves
the pattering of boys' feet
through the built canyons
of the past. I have heard

such singing. The mocking-bird
has sung for me. Each day
the waters of that sea
are rising blindly to the full.

Decoys

(for John Davies, of Prestatyn)

1

They work in garages,
in cold sheds behind houses,
in basements under harsh lights,
the men who make decoys.

At desks, or behind
the wheels of trucks,
all day their hands have ached
for this. They eat slowly,

savour their last cups,
and in a dream, breath
masked from the snuff of wood,
go now to set the false birds

free. Their saws are warm
and humming, their burrs
their files, rotate
at an electric wish.

Everywhere is a fur
of dust; of walnut,
of white oak, logged forests
dried for this making.

With the flat of their palms
they measure the neck's right curve
and set with an eye
an angle to the beak.

Such birds must look comfortable.
The glass eyes are inserted
in a parody of safety,
neither wild nor mad.

Now it is the caress
of repetitive fine abrasives
transforms the annual rings
to feathers, to a persuasion of down.

The paint is brilliant,
quick-drying, acrylic,
more accurate than nature.
It is touched with shadows.

There are seven shades of black.

2

Such perfect creatures keep
at the edges of your mind.
They will not breed, are mere
flawless images. Let them bob
in the ebb of your knowledge.

Soon you will forget them.
White-fronts out of Spitzbergen,
flying through sleet cold enough
to freeze the soft tongues in their mouths,
would find your decoys faulty.

Yet you can tease them down
with a sheet of newsprint,
torn like a heart and weighted
with a clod of grass. Set it
blunt end to the wind, and watch

the great birds from the sea
come flighting in. But the best,
the most killing, of all deceits
is a dead bird. Keep the few
unbroken of your last deaths. Place them

pale breasts to the sky, heads
to the wind, and let them lie
on the cold saltings,
on scatterings of snow no whiter
than the fans of their tails.

Do this alone, on a night
no other man would walk in,
wary of ice in your gun-barrels,
the tide shifting, the light
blown all ways of the compass.

You must be still as a dead bird.

3

The gun has its knowledge, its action
fast as instinct. Once, on an empty night,
our sacks still folded, a heavy dew
an hour away with the dawn,
my gun swung in its own smooth curve,
pulling my hands to fire.
There was not a pause.

And the mallard fell out of the darkness,
in its weight, its feathered heaviness.
It was a green drake. I took it from the ditch
as it eye faded. By god, said my friend, dancing,
You scraped it off the face of the moon.
I brushed the wing that had pushed night from under it.

It was the gun had known.

204

4

There are men, they are born with it,
who have the gift of calling.

They live in cottages on the saltings,
or if in villages, move quietly by night.

Nothing changes in their country but they know it;
the angle of a gate, a dropped branch, shifts of the wind.

For them the sky fills with wildfowl. The lines of flight
clamour for them, for them sanderling

and redshank patter at the tide's withdrawing runnels.
They turn, in quiet beds, at a flake of snow.

When they call, when they squat in a hide
or hide in a thick of bush,

they blow through cupped hands
for a meeting of birds and animals.

Call again and again, the note rising,
an elegy for vulnerable creatures,

the hare, the partridge, runners and low fliers.
And for the waterbirds, for rafts of teal,

for pied shelduck, for skeins of geese,
brent goose, snow goose, pinkfoot, Canada,

the little bean goose, hardy in the air,
the royal swan, the whooper,

all humble on land, on their pliable webs.
Let the men put away rapacious lead, let them be still.

The birds have given them the wide, cold sky.
They have given them dreams of innocence.

They have given them voices.

New Poems, 1996

Borders

(i.m. John Ormond, died May 4th 1990)

The border I knew best was halfway over
the bridge between the town and Breconshire.
Beneath,
              the river's neutral water
moved on
              to other boundaries.

I walked the bridge each Saturday, stopped
at a guessed measure,
lived a moment in adventurous limbo.
Did I stand on air then, invisibly
taken to some unknown world, some nowhere?
Where was I then? I was whole
but felt an unseen line
divide me, send my strong half forward,
keep my other timidly at home.

I have always lived that way,
crossed borders resolutely
while looking over my shoulder.

Not long ago
driving in America
in high cold desert country below the Rockies,
I saw at the roadside
parked on an acre open as the moon,
a ring of shabby cars
old Chevies and Caddies,
some prosperous trucks.
The Indians were showing on folding tables
their ceremonial silver, heavy necklaces, rich
with turquoise and hammered squash-blossom, oval
silver bangles.

                    Navajo and Zuni,
old tribes, hardy and skilled.
They stood behind their work in the flat wind,
not smiling.
I love the things they make,
haggled for a buckle for my belt,
silver, a design
rayed like the cold sun,
and, walking away, saw
cut into the concrete
the meeting place of four states.
Crouched there, I placed a foot in Utah,
a foot in Arizona, my palms flat
in the dust of Colorado and New Mexico.

Restless as dust, scattered.

A man I knew, my old friend,
moved out as I did, but returned,
followed his eyes and crossed the borders
into his own country. When he left,
it was to see his place from a distance
and peacefully go home. The world grew small
for him, to one country, a city, a house.

His mother, calmly and nobly dying,
asked on her last day for champagne
which she had never tasted. She wet her lips,
and in the evening called into her room
someone unseen. 'Who would have thought it,'
she said, very clearly, and crossed the border
for which all others are a preparation.

And Sally Taylor, her mother dying in the next room,
heard women's voices, young and laughing,
come in to fetch the old lady.

Border, boundary, threshold, door —
Orpheus moved either way, the living and the dead
were parted by a thin reflection
he simply walked through. But who can follow?

For all the boundaries I have crossed, flown over,
knowingly, unknowingly, I have no answers;
but sit in the afternoon sun, under mountains
where stale snow clings in shadowy patches,
remember my friend, how he had sung,
hope he is still singing.

Bridal Veil Falls, Early Winter

The season's freeze has locked the waterfall,
its wavering fluid, into a cold permanence.
The last arcs of free spray, crystalised
in mid-air, are scattered among the stones.
Here is a preserved droplet, a Victorian stopper,
which will not melt for months. Water is held,
as these lines hold under the bite of words.
The wind is the one sound, hissing
into the crevice over the quiet ice.

For seventy hardening seasons I've watched
the stopping of waterfalls. Some of the time
I knew and perhaps understood how water
changed in winter, what happened to molecules,
how the structures of elements could petrify
in a night from bounding liquid to
an obdurate smoothness. Not any longer.
All that's confusing now. I am content
to watch the world turn cold with its old grace.

Soon younger men will come, active, dressed
against ice, with crampons and pitons, coils
of nylon rope, looking up quite differently
from the river bed. They'll wear their red
windproofs on the pallor of the ice,
search for fingerhold and toehold, secure
their spiked boots, begin to climb.
It's grim work. At first one sees them progress
with a quick elegance, straight up, few overhangs.

But soon they must steady, take the ice axe
from its holster, with brisk hacks
of the blade cut steps out of the sliding
fall, blocks of cold spoil dropping
to the valley floor, skittering down.
They'll pull themselves up to the line
of sky above them, the canyon's edge.
What then? No axe will chop footholds
in that thin air. They won't fly, I can tell them.

Owen Sullivan and the Horse

He has had bronchitis and sits now
In the sunlight, on a yellow cushion
His mother has put on the doorstep.
Across the street is the stable,
With stalls for two horses, where
Ernie Jenkins keeps his single pony.
He can hear the weight of the horse.

Once he was afraid of horses, but
Ernie Jenkins lifted him in the air
And he sat on the pony's back, and
Felt it breathing. The brown hair
Was hard and straight against his knees.

He held his fist full of the coarse mane.
It was then he knew at once about horses.

And he looked down from his height
Seeing his mother looking up at him,
Smiling, although he was so far away,
And he said, 'I'm sorry for horses,
They have no hands and they can't talk.
They don't have any time to play and
They live in the dark of the stable.'

But Ernie Jenkins laughed and swung him down.
He is worried now about the clumsiness
Of the pony's feet, and its pure eyes.
Owen Sullivan has left his house, walks
Royally up the street towards the child.
Unhurried, his long Irish face unshaved
And noble, he wears the fringes of his rags

With simple arrogance. He looks down.
The child stares from his yellow cushion.
He knows this is a serious moment.
'You can hear the horse,' Owen Sullivan says.
The boy points. 'He's in the stable.'
Together they wait, man and boy, for the
Proper moment. 'Remember this,' unbending

Owen says, 'Do not forget this, boy,
Only fools and horses work.' And turns,
Alone in the world and wise. And walks away.
In easy warmth the boy closes his eyes.
Sleep hums in his ears, but he can distinguish
The serene and airy footsteps of Owen Sullivan,
The pony's stumbling iron on the stable cobbles.

Bringing in the Selves

Eight years old, he loves water,
knows streams, lakes,
the separate vegetations
of still and moving waters,
he has marked them turn brown
the few seasons of his winters.

He has in his mind
the names of waterbirds,
mallard, swan, moorhen;
he discovers and murmurs
their incantatory syllables.

He counts shadows of trout
hovering in water.

In a miracle of April
he walks by the river
collecting with his eyes
what the weather brings.

Mild rain polishes
the skins of new leaves.

A visitation of swallows,
wet, exhausted,
drops out of the hot countries.

Among white raindrops
they cling to the twigs
of a leafless birch tree.
Vulnerable warm bundles,
red-throated,
they flick their glossy wings,
do not fly
from the boy's unmoving intensity.

He holds every feather
in his memory, in the diffused
light shining
through waterdrops.

Warm air carries
the boy's regard
for the swallows,
for the little tree,
black nubs ready for leafing.

Come in, child, come in.
The circle is made.

The Night Before the Game

When night comes early and darkness
fills the streets, all the way
from the cold road past roofs and chimneys
to the colder stars, he takes
his tennis ball to the circle of light
beneath the street lamp. And begins. He taps
the ball from one foot to the other, walks
it about the iron standard, patting it
with deft little directives of his shoes,
never letting it out of his easy reach,
as Con Holland had taught him.

Now he is trotting, the ball
two smooth inches from his toes,
never getting away, never breaking
the rhythm of the circle
around the lamp-post. And he
dances after it, swaying from side
to side, feinting with hips and shoulders

so that imaginary tacklers sprawl
behind him, and the little
grey ball veers minutely
in its steady circling as he steers
and strokes it.

        'Be in control,'
Con Holland had said, 'Keep the ball
with you, protect it, push it and pat it,
left foot and right foot'.

          So he runs around
in the ring of light, a small thin boy,
until his running is automatic and the ball's
response is to something other than his feet,
something different, a sudden unity,
a harmony, like happiness.

Knowing he can do anything,
he pounces two-footed, traps
the ball between his feet, throws it
a yard in front of him, and lofts
its bounce head high, holds it a moment
on his forehead, allows it to drop
to his lifted thigh, pause, and fall,
soft as a mouse, to the ground.
He repeats this again and again, until
it is perfect beyond anticipation.

And goes home.

       Although it is dark
he can almost see his white shorts
folded on the bedside chair, with
his new stockings. His shirt, red
with gold sleeves, is on a hanger
behind the door. He is straight
and calm in his sheets. His bed
is flat as a field.

'Be aware', Con Holland had warned,
'of every man on the field. Protect
the ball, move it safely. Know
where everybody is. And best of all,
know the spaces between them.
Keep the ball until you know those spaces.
Push the ball at exact speeds
into spaces your men can run to fill.'

Almost asleep, he imagines the green game
in the morning, how the ball will roll
into the spaces between his friends,
intricately connecting them,
a web, a moving thread of playing.

And on the touchline fathers and brothers
and people who leave their cars
to watch boys play soccer, they too
have their spaces, move into them,
shouting their support.

And behind them are the spaces of their homes,
the places they work, the places of travelling,
all to be filled, people moving at exact speeds,
all intricately connected.

              Arthur Ferguson,
who's gone to Australia, there's a huge space.

           We are connected,
he thinks, turning into the warm darkness,
we are all the same.

A Grain of Sand

(What commerce, what intimacy had I had, until then, with
Empedocles' four elements?
        Primo Levi, *The Periodic Table*)

A thin boy is standing
not at rest
in the pool of his shadow.

He is touching
the surface
of a stone wall

with his fingers.

Now the flat of his hand.

Startled, he realises
he has against his palm
the bulk of the whole world,

the growth and decay of stone,
the age of mountains.

Loose grains lodge
in the ridges of his skin
and fall minutely
to the ground.

Everything falls
to the claiming earth.

If air were supportive,
if it could hold unmoving
even those flecks of stone,
then his brother
needing only one foot on the ground

as he springs and runs
would use the air as fish use water,
would fly.

But this boy
will sing the earth.

Now he becomes earth.

He holds in the cavities
of his life
the air of space

and breathes
to the four corners of the world
his sudden understanding.

Elemental gases explode
for him
in the burning of the sun

and the fiery stars,

and little universes grow
in their silences
in their exhausted cooling.

He will sing the earth.

He sees the moist edges of rivers
the tidemarks of beaches
where subtle water

is at work
on the placid earth.

He will sing the earth,
its textures and tiered strata,

the quick lives of its surfaces
and arriving cities, built
with climbing labour.

He names the solid properties
of house, tree, petal, friend,
gives a voice to love,
peoples the earth
with the nouns of his insight.

Earth, air, fire, water;
a little of each,
to comfort life
and define death.

He is moving away,
his feet slow on the hot ground.

He knows where he walks.

Spitfire

'Flight Sergeant (Pilot) John Curtis Bevan, 1314667, serving
with the Royal Air Force (Volunteer Reserve) 611 Squadron,
died on 9th November 1943, age 21, and is buried in Plot 4,
Row AA, Grave 17, in Longuenesse (St Omer) Cemetery,
France.' — excerpt from a letter from the Commonwealth
War Graves Commission.

The Spitfire One
is made by Vickers Armstrong
in Southampton, Winchester, Swindon,
cities the three boys have not seen.
Each month in the library
they search *Flight's* newest pages
for images of its symmetry, perfect
beyond eagles, thirty feet long.

Wearing incongruous floats
it wins The Schneider Trophy,
sweeping in tightest bends
above a riptide
breaking against The Needles.
They speak its language,
having learned by heart this rune:
one 1030-hp Rolls-Royce Merlin
V12 liquid-cooled engine:
maximum speed 355 mph, range
three hundred and ninety-five miles.
But in their minds
its flight is silent.
They imagine it through the air
with their gliding hands.
Their cycles race above clouds.

They do not think of this:
armament, *four 7.7-mm. machine-guns,*
two 20-mm. cannons,
not even as they grow
into men's long bodies,
manage their cracking voices,
learn that innocence ends.

On a wide beach
at the edge of Europe,
the sun going down,
they throw a football
above their running shadows.
As they twist and catch
the sand is granular
between their toes.

It is the last evening of peace.

The tide is ebbing.

The beach is dark as plums
and heavy with water.

In Cefn Cemetery

In Cefn Cemetery
          he is the eldest son,
his dignity a gift
          of the cold blood.
He has ridden in the first car
          behind the coffin
with his brothers
          and his father's brothers.
In a bowed circle
          of serious men
he stands attentive
          to the rituals of burial.
In their dark suits
          they are as strangers to him.
He has recognised their sympathy.

          Nothing is real,
not the pointed evergreens,
          not their heavy branches,
not the frail grasses, bent
          in pulses of the wind.
One after the other
          he broods on their attitudes.
He will never forget them.

          Stupid with grief,
his brother is leaving.
          He will climb the rock face
beneath Morlais Castle,
          challenge with his life
the indifferent stones.
          Hanging in the wind
by his broken fingernails
          the boy weeps as he learns
the futility of his anger.

But the eldest son walks
            in the tiredness of evening;
lifting his head
            finds nobody in front of him.

In the City

In the city he has forgotten how to be alone.
He is often astonished by the silence of libraries,
In the tall buildings he admires and visits, he
whistles sometimes, from nervousness.
He stands before paintings, studying eloquence.
Not wanting simplicity, he imagines life
as sauntering from room to room, not aware
that he runs everywhere, across
Royal Crescent where he pats the black labrador,
up Lansdowne Hill to the Racecourse,
among fashionable shoppers
in Gay Street and Milsom Street.
On Sundays he reads *The Observer*
in the Botanical Gardens where sat
the sailor's ghost. (In his own house
a dead admiral walks at evening,
meticulous and gentlemanly,
decants his shadowy claret.)

They walk in October evenings
when surprising cold
suddenly drops the beech leaves
and mist fills the bowl of hills.
Their hidden feet
are muffled to brushing echoes.
He does not think to say out loud
that she is as new bread to him,
as air and daylight, his certainty and life.

Her face is the one he looks for
in all the brilliant streets.
Hand in hand they walk home
through autumn mists.

In darkness beyond night
he runs downhill to the Post Office.
Flattening rain has emptied the world.
Nothing is alive.

From the roof of the City Building
a little screech owl screams
and screams again,
helpless in daunting storm,
small and desperate in the downpour.

Hid in the lee of a door
he looks toward the bird.
He too is helpless.
He is blind with rain,
Not an inch of his skin is dry.

In the lash and whip of downpour,
bent double, he climbs the hill,
the hoarse voice of water, the gutters flooded.

It is not the rain
makes him shiver.

A Round Table

The young man is crouched
over a roundel of wood.
He has sawn two rough semi-circles
from the seat of an old school desk,
the grain hard and intractable,
fighting the teeth.

With hot glue from the pot
he has joined the trued surfaces.
Clamped for a week, they
are wedded together.

He feels with his hand
the flaws in his planing
and with a piece of broken glass,
blue glass, tracing its shadow,
he lifts from the surface
a sliver so thin
yellow light comes through it.

He will shape the circumference
with spokeshave and glasspaper
to the line of his compass.
With labour and time,
awkwardly, without skill,
he will finish the little table
to give to his wife.

Seven months in the making,
forty years ago.

I am bringing in the selves.
I am calling him home.

Journeying in Ithaca

Journeying in Ithaca
in his old age,
he climbs to the town of Stavros.

He walks among olive trees
in the dusty gardens.

Early mist covers the sea.

Odysseus is home,
atop his column.

Stone head of Odysseus,
dry moss in his eye,
stares over two concrete houses,
a wrecked Honda.

He records with his Leica
the face of the demi-god,
thinks of the men,
wherever their fortune,
who turn their faces
to the fires of home.

White sunlight lifts the mist.
The sea begins to juggle
its silver platters.

In that blinding dazzle
he sees with clarity
Ithaca vanishing.

Snow King and Ice Queen

Now the days are very short,
    The nights are cold.
Snow and ice are our domain.
    The world grows older.

There's a fire burns in the ice,
    Blood burns in the snow.

Our eyes give colour to the skies
     As we grow older.

You give yourself to me,
     I give myself to you.
We together are the world
     As we grow older.

i.m. Reverend Lawrence Scanlan, DD,
1843-1915, First Bishop of Salt Lake

He was a boy in a green country, dressed
in plain homespun, his wrinkled stockings
about his ankles as he trod the fields,
Paddy Scanlan's fat fields, a hundred acres.

There was water everywhere, the Suir
coming down through Thurles, its unnamed
tributaries never failing, the grass
growing tall, and the small black cattle

up to their stomachs in it. He was
a strong boy, as good as a man,
but that he had an eye above
the springing ditches, an ear

open for more than the commands of the farm.
Was it in May, when the hedges
were opulent with the white froth
of Queen Anne's Lace and the last swag

of hawthorn turned brown over them,
that God called to him out of the leaves?
Did God tell him then that man's home
was not a house, but a travelling road

he must walk the whole of his days?
Well, he walked the one road of the Golden Vale
and saw the sacred wells hung with
ragged prayers, and the little holy

buildings of petitions and miracles
holding up against the centuries.
Larry Scanlan was a strong boy, tall,
he walked the road through the schools

of Thurles seminary, and All Hallows
in Dublin. It was a straight road.
It led him, a collared priest, to the boat.
It was, for him, a long road out of Ireland.

Nor was the turn and thrust of the tide
enough to distract him, nor the brief days
in New York. When he stepped off the hot quay
at Aspinwall, in the Isthmus of Panama,

among dark people, he may have thought
of the Wexmore children, waving their coloured
ribbons from a green hill as the Irish Mail
nosed out of Rosslare; but he faced

into his work, he was well trained.
He toiled in the roads of San Francisco,
in the spoil of Nevada goldfields, his head
higher than any. Twenty-five years old

he came into Utah, gaunt, shivering
with the mountain fever. 'A plain man,
not highly gifted', said the historian.
But a man grows into his gifts

and if his speech was terse, each word
was chosen. He came in the summer
of 1873, gathering the little church,
ninety people out of the whole city,

around him. Father Scanlan, a young man,
waiting at the mine gates on pay days
for the gift of a few coins to keep open
his church doors, at his prayers

in the room behind the cold
hall where year by year his flock
multiplied. The city grew. Grew
prosperous. Wide streets, heavy

well-founded buildings, offices, shops,
all the aspirations of business
spread out beneath the cold eye
of the desert hawk. A practical man,

Father Scanlan grew with the State.
No horseman, he rode where Escalante
and Dominguez had ridden, over the
arid land. Became a linguist, bending

his soft brogue to the service
of German immigrants. Built
schools and hospitals. Left
sturdy evidence of his mission

in the churches of his travelling,
in Ogden, in Eureka, all along
the Wasatch Front, in small stations
founded at hopeful settlements

where a few met together. And,
forty-three years old, named
Bishop, he recognised the proper time
for a great house of his faith.

Men build cathedrals out of their humility,
wishing to praise God with their skill;
out of arrogance, at having imagined
unimaginable God; out of an exercise

of strength, thinking that stone is harder
and stronger than time; out of the wish
to pass down to new generations evidence
of their belief; out of a need

to have for their prayers a heart,
and a place fit for their veneration.
Cathedrals are built of what materials
God gives to us for the purpose.

On the Pacific island of Chiloe the cathedral
is built of corrugated sheeting,
its metal painted a ferocious orange,
against the onslaughts of weather

and as a statement of joy. But I am a man
from Europe's edge and have seen
Salisbury and Winchester, calm monuments,
lift grey stone to grey clouds. The boy Scanlan

could have walked from his father's house
to the Rock of Cashel, and every step
those towers holy for a thousand years
would have been in his eyes. Limestone

out of Munster quarries made them.
So Bishop Scanlan would build his cathedral
of tactful sandstone, his altar of
brown marble from central Utah, God

having provided such things. But stone
is a slow weight, made in God's own time
out of the bones of spent oceans,
and heavy to raise. He was sixty-six

when he passed at last in procession
through the wide doors opened for him,
he in his ermine, and on his hand
the ancient ring of the great men of Cashel.

Sixty-six years old, a man powerful
in himself and endowed with power.
He had entered the Cathedral
of St Mary Magdalene, he sat enthroned.

Six years he ruled this house, turning
gentler, the strong man; growing
more silent, the man of few words;
watching the seasons change, the man of action.

In May snow released its water to the valleys
and careful husbandmen, standing in orchards,
trickled the channeled streams about the roots
of their apple trees. Their branches carried

the weightless purity of blossom, white
promise. The city basked in renewal.
And what was earth of Lawrence Scanlan
was laid to rest in the Cathedral,

is buried here. Where else would we honour
his long bones? Where else should we listen
for memories of his voice, in the echoes
and whispers behind the verities of the mass?

Peaches

In his life he has made seven gardens, two
from the untilled meadow, some in good heart
after the spades of other men. One, unkempt
inside its formal Georgian walls, he brought
to perfect order out of wilderness, its geometric
beds to flower, renewed its lawn, cut back
its gnarled espaliers and clipped their trimmed limbs
to the limestone. He remembers the rough bark

of those old varieties, pears mostly, and how
he hit the supporting nails into the mortar.

This is the first time he has grown a peach tree.
It is the third year of the small tree's bearing,
and already his black dog has cleared the lowest
bough of its green fruit, nibbled the flesh,
left a scatter of kernels about the grass. No matter,
there's plenty. He has posted a stout cross
beneath the branches, else a heavy harvest of peaches
pulls the whole bush down. Watching the early blossom
has been his pleasure, the frail brevity of blossom
blown in cold weather, then the incipient fruit.

He does not walk in the garden until evening,
the days too hot for his uncovered head. When shadows
spread from under the trees, he stands there,
near a dusty lilac, surprised by hot gusts
out of the desert. His roses are abundant now.
He has let them grow and mingle, throwing their trails
over and through the massed green of other shrubs.
Alba and gallica roses, damask roses, centifolia roses,
an old moss rose, a bed of hardy rugosa. Refreshed
by roses, he cherishes the garden air, his head filled

with generations of perfume. Far in his life,
he nods to the spent iris, remembering how in water
his yellow flags stood high, how as a child he took
in his father's garden bright vegetables from the soil,
and how in the autumn hedge blackberries glowed.
It is his way of life to desert his gardens.
The neighbour's evening lamps light up the peaches.
Fruit is ripening, orchards everywhere ripen.
He throws a fallen peach to his black dog.
The animals were not expelled from Eden.

His Father, Singing

My father sang for himself,
out of sadness and poverty;
perhaps from happiness,
but I'm not sure of that.

He sang in the garden,
quietly, a quiet voice
near his wallflowers
which of all plants

he loved most, calling them
gillyflowers, a name
learned from his mother.
His songs came from a time

before my time, his boy's
life among musical brothers,
keeping pigeons, red and blue
checkers, had a racing cycle

with bamboo wheels. More often
he sang the songs he'd learned,
still a boy, up to his knees
in French mud, those dying songs.

He sang for us once only,
our mother away from the house,
the lamp lit, and I reading,
seven years old, already bookish,

at the scrubbed table.
My brother cried from his crib
in the small bedroom, teething,
a peremptory squall, then a long

wail. My father lifted from
the sheets his peevish child,
red-faced, feverish, carried
him down in a wool shawl

and in the kitchen, holding
the child close, began to sing.
Quietly, of course, and swaying
rhythmically from foot to foot,

he rocked the sobbing boy.
I saw my brother's head,
his puckered face, fall
on my father's chest. His crying

died away, and I
read on. It was my father's
singing brought my head up.
His little wordless lullabies

had gone, and what he sang
above his baby's sleep
was never meant
for any infant's comfort.

He stood in the bleak kitchen,
the stern, young man, my father.
For the first time raised
his voice, in pain and anger

sang. I did not know his song
nor why he sang it. But stood
in fright, knowing it important,
and someone should be listening.

Acknowledgements

Acknowledgements for some of the previously uncollected poems in this volume are due to *The Atlantic Monthly*, *The New Criterion*, *The Sewanee Review*, *Epoch*, *Literature and Belief*, *Tar River Poetry*, *Gulf Coast*, *Poetry Wales* and *Drawing Down the Moon* (Seren, 1995).

The other poems in collected in this volume originally appeared in: *The Loud Winter* (1967), *Finding Gold* (1967), *Ransoms* (1970), *Mountains Polecats Pheasants* (1974), *Water Voices* (1980), and *A Sea in the Desert* (1989).

The Author

Leslie Norris was born in Merthyr Tydfil in 1921. Formerly a teacher and headmaster, he has for many years taught literature and creative writing in American universities, most recently at Brigham Young, Utah, where he was Christiansen Professor of Poetry.

He has been writing poetry since 1941 and has published ten collections, including a *Selected Poems*. This *Collected Poems* celebrates Leslie Norris's seventy-fifth year and his return to Wales, and is the companion volume to his *Collected Stories*.